My Story

TRAGEDY TURNED TO OPPORTUNITY

My Story

TRAGEDY TURNED TO OPPORTUNITY

by Dr. Lillie M. Coley, PhD

Contact Local Book store or Call:

KWJ Publishing
609-225-6357
or

Write:

P.O. Box 203
Blackwood, NJ 08012
www.drlil.com   ceo1@mail.com

**Check Website for up to date contact
information.**

Unless otherwise indicated, all scriptures quotations are taken from the King James Version of the Bible or the New International Version. The word *Church* in this book is capitalized on purpose based on teachings from seminaries.

All family photos are the property of Dr. Coley.

ISBN: 0-9714786-0-0
Copyright 2001, 2003, 2007 by
Dr. Lillie M. Coley, PhD

Published by:
KWJ Publishing
P.O. Box 203
Blackwood, NJ 08012 USA

Acknowledgments

To God My Father, who is my Lord and Savior, my Friend, my Companion, my Everything—who told Me in a small still voice to go forth with this. I stepped out on faith!

Thanks

Editing

Jean Currie Church (Howard University),
Other CEO Associates

Publishing Support

Myra Queen

Book Layout

CEO & Associates

Book Cover

Left Hand Graphic Inc., Eric Oliver

This book is dedicated to the late and the great James Odell Coley, Sr., my beloved father and Lillie Charlene Coley, my beloved Mother.
and
My family

Contents

Chapter 1

Experiencing Shock In Childhood

The day of the funeral was one I will never forget. Whenever God allows tragedy to strike, it is for a reason. The Lord foreknew that my father was not going to change. He also knew that my father thought he owned his family. This is what he was taught, but this was wrong.

Before the funeral, our family had many reporters and people coming to our house for our story. It really did not make any sense. People from all over the world sent us money, clothes, cards, toys, and other household items. Because our family was well known, the funeral attendance was expected to be big. Planning was so that the family would not suffer too much; inconvenience was the key. I remember different people taking my siblings and I to stores to get clothes and shoes for the funeral. To this day, I have no idea who they were. So many knew my mother because she helped them with their problems, and they felt indebted to her.

Often, we would be told, "You kids have nothing to be ashamed of. Your mother helped so many people." My mother planted a lot of seeds in helping others. When you help you never know what life is going to bring to you and those around you.

When the funeral cars came to the house to get us, I felt my stomach drop, because this would be the last day I would see the apple of my eye and the first man I ever loved. Our church could hold about three thousand people in the main sanctuary and balcony. The entire downstairs was filled, and there were some people in the balcony. During the funeral, my mind was in wonderland. I could not believe that this was happening. You could not hear anything during the service because somebody was always crying. My brothers, sisters, and I were in the first row just sobbing away. This was a double funeral. My mother's casket was right in front of us and my father's right next to hers. This was truly the worst day of my life.

As I reflect on that day now, it seems hard to see how anything good could come out of so much pain. But somehow in God's infinite wisdom and divine love, He turned this whole tragedy into an opportunity later in our lives. As a matter of fact, while Reverend Leon H. Sullivan was doing the eulogy, he said, *"Turn this tragedy into an opportunity."*

One never knows why things happen in life. Some people get cancer, other experience teenage pregnancy, rape, or molested. As I meet people every day, it seems everybody has a story to tell about what they have gone through or what they are going through. I must say our parents' death was our tragedy. People must remember that God did not cause this to happen, but He allowed it to happen. He knows the end from the beginning. Even in something as horrible as death, God wanted to show Himself in a big way—and He did.

Emotionally none of the young children were able to make it through the funeral or to the burial. Friends of my parents took Yvette, Annette, Kurt, Michelle, and me home. My older siblings did go to the burial site to see our parents' final resting place.

Our house was packed with many people after the funeral. Some were just overly curious and wanted to see how immaculately my mother's house was kept. The house was so crowded that a table had to be used to secure the kitchen area from visitors. I could not eat a thing. I wanted my parents back and nothing else. I found that when people are going through a tragedy or crisis, others will use this as an opportunity to take advantage of the situation. Many people stole items from our house such as pots and pans and other household items. It was truly unbelievable.

No one can really imagine the impact my parents' death had on my siblings. For me I felt emotionally drained with no life or energy. This whole ordeal produced the shock of our lives. If we had witnessed our parents in an abusive relationship, it would have been easier to digest but we never saw our parents argue until the last year of their lives, and we never heard them use foul language. We did not see any of that. We only knew that one minute they were alive, and we were living in paradise with the golden rug under our feet, and the next minute they were gone. It appeared that someone had came along, snatched the rug from under our feet, and left us standing on bare ground. It takes years to build things and seconds to destroy it.

When dealing with shock, our family had to go through its stages and phases to ensure the proper recovery. Usually, one must first come to terms with the situation, but in our case, we understood what happened but just could not figure out why. This conservative and all-American family had no answers, just a lot of questions. All of us received counseling afterward and we had to talk about it. This, of course, helped, but it was difficult. We were forced to talk. At this point, it started to sink in, but not at first.

Although all these things were taking place, God did not say anything to me during my time in prayer with Him. It seemed like there was a holy hush; the heavens were silent. But how many of you know that just because God is not talking does not mean He is not there with you? During this time, He didn't talk. He only listened. While He was only listening, He carried me and my family in His precious arms for comfort and strength. It is truly miraculous how God kept my family together in every aspect of our lives: spiritually, financially, emotionally, and morally. Of course, all of these areas were not perfect, but for children with no parents, God definitely showed that He was in control. He allowed the tragedy to happen, but the devil was not allowed to touch any of us.

It is truly unbelievable how God kept us together. We were never separated and had no real major problems growing up. I am not bragging. I am just thankful. Some families I know with two parents have had more problems than I had with all my sisters and brothers combined. Of course, this is not a comparison contest, but this is a demonstration of God's sovereignty, power, and divine order over our family. "All things truly do work together for good for those who love the Lord and are called according to His purpose." (Romans 8:23, NIV)

I need to mention also that all my brothers and sisters were "saved," or Christians before my parents died. I was saved at nine years old. My mother can take credit for this; she made sure we attended Church regularly and were exposed to spiritual events and activities. From this we would have encounters with God that would lead to salvation. God designed all this. He knew we were going to need Him as a foundation in order to survive the tragedy of our parents' death. I became very active in the Church at the age of nine and this continued into my adult life.

Chapter 2

Fairy Tale Childhood

I was born into a middle-class family to James O. Coley, Sr., and Lillie C. Coley. When my parents met, my mother was a model. She had won several beauty contests, and the camera definitely loved her face, but she gave all that up to be with my father. My mother had four children from a previous marriage, and my father loved her so much that he took care of these children as if they were his own. Life was not easy for African Americans during the early sixties, but somehow things worked out just fine for us.

My mother had eight additional children from her union with my father. We moved into our new home located in Philadelphia, Pennsylvania, during the mid-sixties. The oldest Coley from my parents' union was five years of age, and the youngest from her previous marriage was sixteen at the time so most of the children in the home with our parents were Coleys. My mother said that we moved into our family home when she was pregnant with me, and this is how she always knew how long we had been living there. We were a family blessed with food, clothing, and other luxuries at a time when our country was considered economically depressed.

During my early childhood, my father, a Marine, would often be gone for months. He wrote often and sent big boxes of candy, and we could hardly wait to hear from him. Since my father didn't want to move us around the country during his civil service, we stayed in Philadelphia. My mother, who did not have to work because Daddy was financially stable, would travel to see him wherever he was stationed.

My father would come home periodically from the military base but every time he had to leave, we would cry like babies. It was really hard to see him go because we adored him and loved the ground he walked on. When he was home, he spent quality time with us. We played games such as the horsy ride, where he would put one of us on his lap or knee, and let us ride him until we fell off. It was always fun to see which one of us would stay on the longest.

My father never seemed to tire of playing with us. He also loved giving us piggyback rides and, my favorite, putting us on his shoulders. And, no matter what the weather, he gave us ice cream cones. His favorite was Breyer's or Sealtest Butter Pecan. Daddy also would bring home gourmet cheeses from all over the world for my mother, especially during her pregnancies. So, all of us came into this world loving cheese and ice cream.

One day my brother Odell and I asked our father if he could come home to stay like a regular dad. My father had a very soft spot for his children, and we could get him to do just about anything. He talked it over with my mother, and he retired from the military a year later. Boy, we were happy to see our daddy every day! Once my daddy came home, I could not even fall asleep at night unless he was in the house. I would be in the bed half asleep until I heard his voice, then I would fall sound asleep.

My dad would turn off all the lights before he and my mother went to bed and come and watch us sleep. One time, I could feel his presence, and I woke up. Everything was dark, so I reached out to feel for him, and there he was. I asked him about it the next day, and he told me it was not him. He denied this with a smile until the day he died, but I knew it was him.

Even after my dad retired he still worked part-time. When his shifts would change, we would not see him some mornings because he had to leave early. I said to him, "I want to see you in the morning." He said, "You're going to have to get up early to see me," so I did. I do not know how I did, but I knew exactly when to get up. I would sit on his lap, and eat breakfast with him. That time with him was so special to me. I can still remember this clearly, even today. After getting up so early, I would be tired the rest of the day, and my mother soon told me to stay in the bed and get my sleep.

Our house, as I remember, was very big and beautiful. We were the only African American family in our neighborhood. We were surrounded by neighbors who were Caucasian people of Jewish descent. Jewish people owned and operated every store. My mother was overly protective of us and kept us in the house ninety-five percent of the time. Since we were in the house, our father made the it our haven by providing us a play area in the basement.

In thinking back about our house, which my family still owns today, I remember that our living room had deep royal-blue carpet with a big red diamond in the middle.

The living room held a love seat, sofa, long stereo, floor-model color TV, and a fireplace. Our dining room could seat sixteen people, with other furniture against the wall. My mother's kitchen was her pride and joy. Everything had to be sky blue, her favorite color. The kitchen had a washer, a big freezer, a side-by-side refrigerator, a dishwasher, long countertops, a lazy susan, and a big table that would seat eight people.

Our backyard was also big. First our backyard had swings and sliding boards, but later our father told us he wanted to get a pool. Daddy could swim like a fish. He just loved the water, and so did I. I inherited most of his habits, although he taught all of us how to swim. Before we got the pool, Daddy took us to a clean public pool called Gustin Lake every day during the summer. I think he got tired of going to the public pool, so he bought us one and took down the swings and sliding boards. He purchased a huge above-ground pool big enough for him to swim in. During this time we got our first African American neighbor who was very jealous of my father and my family because we had more than he did. The neighbor often told my brothers, sisters, and me not to play around his house. He would say, "Go get into your pool." We had the pool several years, and all the kids on the block spent a lot of time at our house. They were either in the basement which covered the entire length of the house, shooting pool or swimming in the backyard.

Unfortunately, someone started punching holes in the pool at night, and my father would have to patch them up. Daddy tried to keep up the pool. He sat in it late one night hoping he would catch the person responsible, but no one came. After the third or fourth act of vandalism, Daddy had to take the pool down. We all cried ourselves to sleep that night. My parents considered moving because we were starting to get more African Americans in the neighborhood who did not want to see others with more than they had. Today, we call this jealousy. I learned early about this type of spirit or behavior and from where the saying "pulling each other down like crabs in a barrel" came.

The basement was where we socialized. On one side my father put a pool table, a ping-pong table, and pinball machine. He also built a bathroom for my siblings and me. On the other side, which was considered the girls' side, we had our kitchen set and other items needed to play house. Often, my sisters and I had our daddy come down to have tea and cake. It was funny to see him try to sit in those little chairs. He was a big man, and he had to kneel on the floor to play house with us. After he got up, he would say, "My knees hurt."

The upstairs of our home had four bedrooms, three of which were very large. My sister Shirl and I had the back room, which had a full-size, beautiful white canopy bed that our father bought with all the dressers and mirrors to match. We *loved* our room.

Our brothers, unfortunately, loved the bed, too, and they kept jumping on the canopy top until it finally collapsed. When my mother became pregnant with my sister Michelle, who was the absolute last child, Shirl and I moved to the smaller room. This time our daddy bought us a daybed, and we just loved it, too. Everything about us was big: big family, big house, big car, big meals, and even our thinking was big. Mother always taught her children to think exceedingly and abundantly. She would sometimes say, "Is anything too hard for God?" and we would say, "No, nothing is too hard for God." This became our pattern of thought, and this method became a way of life for our family.

Our home was burglarized by one of the neighbors around the time our pool was destroyed. We were the only family who had a floor-model color TV, an RCA to be exact. My father had also bought us the first TV game called TV Tennis. When our house was robbed, the only thing that was taken was the TV. My father had left a leather jacket on a chair, and there was a radio on the dining room table. The burglar did not want anything else. With all the people in the neighborhood, everyone claimed they saw nothing. Little did they know that my mother had a lot of power in the city, and my parents found out who probably did it. No arrest was ever made due to the lack of evidence. The suspected thief kept the TV in his garage for years because he feared using or selling it since we were the only family with that model. My brother Edward actually saw our property in his garage years later. My father went out the very next day and purchased another color, floor-model TV, and he replaced our wooden front door which was destroyed during the burglary with a white steel one.

After this incident, my brothers, sisters, and I learned a valuable lesson about life and material possessions. It was really hard for some people to survive during those times, but stealing was not the answer to their problem. My mother knew some people who barely had a chair to sit on. She also knew she was fortunate, but until our house was robbed, my brothers, sisters, and I thought everybody lived the way we did.

My father loved family activities, one of which was taking car rides to South Philly to see the planes take off and land. During this time, there was a lot of open space on the side of the road, so we could see the airplane traffic. Every time we crossed the South Philly bridge where the huge oil tanks were, my sister Shirl would get sick from the fumes. We had a challenge of rolling the windows up to keep her from getting sick and still allowing her to see the planes take off and land. We all enjoyed one another within our family circle.

Growing up was a lot of fun. My family had just about everything money could buy and the perfect family setting, but, most of all, we had love from both our parents. We did everything together as a family such as eating, taking walks, and going to the library. In this type of atmosphere, we created a bond that nothing could break, not even death.

My father gave us a good home that was beautiful and immaculate. My mother raised all her children to be clean, to appreciate what we had, and to be mannerable. Mom was very strict, even before Dad came home permanently. We had to go to the library almost every day and read for two hours before we came home. Then it would be homework and dinner. My mother did let us watch some television, but not much. We rarely saw anything on TV after nine, because we were in bed or getting ready for school the next day. We loved the ground my mother walked on. She was a true educator and a very beautiful woman.

It is important for me describe in detail what we had because you cannot miss what you never had. Understanding how we were raised will help you to better understand this book. I think I was between seven and ten years old when most of these events took place. God helped me to remember everything as if it were yesterday. He preserved my memories because He knew that this was all I was going to have, and I would need this information to write this book.

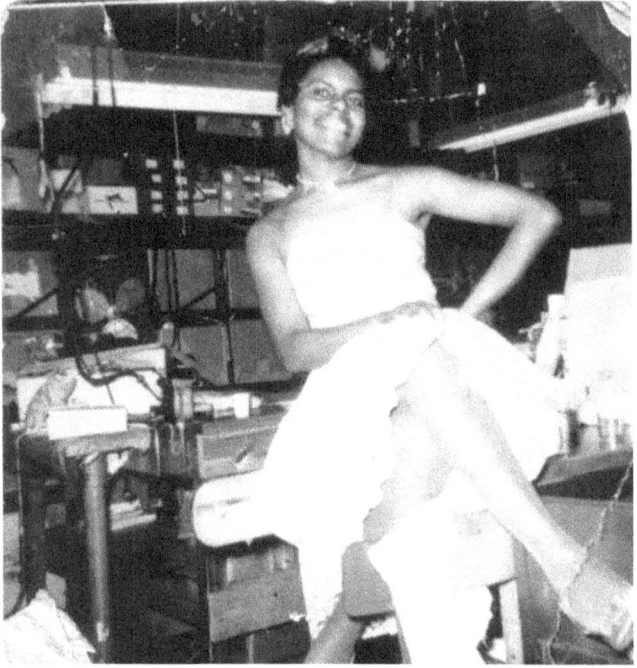

Lillie C. Coley

Chapter 3

The Apple of My Eye and Heart:
My Mother

A s you can see from my mother's picture, she was immaculate. I am not saying this because she was my mommie, but my mother was drop-dead gorgeous. She was extremely health conscious, even from her childhood, and this carried over to her adulthood mainly because her mother died from breast cancer, and because my mother worked as a model in the fashion industry. Her skin was flawless, and she drank water like a fish. She would stand at the sink and drink glass after glass, talking as she drank about how good it tasted. She loved water and vegetables. I think my mother must have given us every vegetable known to mankind. We had two vegetables, one starch, and one meat every night. My father loved meat, so his children picked up this eating habit also. My mother was always flossing her teeth, which were beautiful, and her favorite exercise was walking.

My mother won several beauty contests. She was also an educator and public speaker, but her best role was being our mother. She just loved being a mommie. I remember asking her one day while we were wrestling with my father on the floor, why she had so many children. She said, "Because I loved your father and knew he could take care of us. But, most of all, I always wanted to have a houseful of children and to be able to stay home to raise them." And so she did.

My mother always sent us off to school and was home to receive us every day when we got home. She did not run the streets or go out to nightclubs. She was home every night with us when we went to bed. Often she would visit our schools unexpectedly. I remember one time she visited my classroom, and one the kids nudged me and said, "Your mother's here." I was so scared to turn around, and I wondered what I had done. Later, I found out she did this with my brothers and sisters periodically, so I learned to be on my best behavior because I never knew when I was going to see her.

My mother was the youngest of three sisters who never really had a good relationship with her father, so she enjoyed being married to my dad because he was the fatherly type. My aunts raised her because their mother died when she was only nine years old. My mother and her sisters came from Savannah, Georgia, before they moved to Philadelphia during their late teenage years.

My mother's two sisters had smaller families. My mother breastfed all twelve of her children, and she had midwives deliver almost every one of us. We all were born healthy with all our fingers and toes. My mother did not believe in birth control but she did have an old-fashioned remedy, which she chose not to use. Her sisters did, and that's why their families were so small. I heard they used petroleum jelly. They said nothing would pass through that.

My mother taught my siblings and me important values and that we must believe in ourselves. If there's one thing that she did, it was to teach us that we were s-o-m-e-b-o-d-y. None of my brothers and sisters grew up with low self-esteem. For the most part, each of us felt special and loved. She never let us walk around with our heads down. We were not allowed to look at the ground while walking. Everytime I looked down, she would tap my chin, and say, "Put your head up." After getting your chin tapped and biting your lip, you learned to hold your head up high, but not too high. She taught us to have confidence, not cockiness.

My mother believed not just in being an example, but in setting one. So often in my adult life I have heard people say, "The only example I am going to follow is Jesus," and I think He is a good one to follow but He is sitting on the right hand side of God so the way we live is the best way to represent Jesus, because others are watching. We are the only Bible some people will ever read. People come to Church looking for Jesus, but when they get there, they only find us Christians. So, how we live is, by far, the best teacher.

Often, as my mother was building our character, she used creative ways that I have never forgotten. For instance, when she would bathe us, she would tell us how precious our bodies were and how it was the only thing that we had, so we should take r-e-a-l good care of it. She would say things like, "Don't let nobody touch you in places that are not comfortable to you." These words were lodged within my heart and have helped me become the woman I am today. I know that my body is the most precious thing that I have, and it belongs to *God and me.*

My mother could cook extremely well. We were spoiled. She prepared everything from scratch, and there was a lot of love in her cooking. My father could cook, too, and between the two of them, I do not know who was better. I think my father taught my mother a lot. Mother was a housewife for most of her marriage until she became involved with the community. She became an overnight wonder in politics by providing leadership. I thought my mother was every man's dream. She was beautiful, she could speak extremely well, she had confidence, she was an educator, she believed in and loved people, and she knew how to empower others so they would help themselves. She had us cleaning other people's alleys and streets as part of her political experience.

Our family was my mother's main campaign helpers. My mother ran for committee woman and won. She strongly believed in not giving people a fish but teaching them how to fish. She was the first person I heard use this analogy when I was a young child in the early seventies. That's why she had us cleaning other people's property—to give them the incentive to help themselves. My mother helped many people get jobs and released from jail. As the neighborhood captain and committee woman, she became very well known for helping people. Many frequently called her for assistance with their problems.

My mother basically had a serving spirit. Between my father's duty in the military and my mother's in the community, this spirit spilled over to me. I also have a passion to serve and empower others. My mother just loved people and they loved her. When she talked, others listened. She had the ability to make others feel good about themselves, so everybody was crazy about her.

We had the home everybody wanted to visit and nobody wanted to leave. Sometimes my brothers had to ask visitors if we could go to sleep because it seemed like they were not planning to leave. I have found that people love to be in an atmosphere where their spirit is free.

During the latter part of my mother's life, she still had a strong desire to do other things such as community service. After having so many children, believe it or not, she still had a lot of energy. But, as I mentioned, she had a serving spirit, and these kind of people are not satisfied unless they are helping others. My father did not mind my mother doing community service, as long as it did not take her out of the house for long periods. She started to with sell Amway products when the company first started, and she also sold Tupperware. These two products along with her politics were very successful for her. She really loved selling and using Amway products. Today this company is called Quixtar.

My mother would visit our schools on a semi-routine basis. The teachers and principals all knew her. One day at the school, she saw workers throwing out the excess lunches for the day. She asked, "Why they were throwing out food when there are so many people who are hungry?" The workers told her they had to because it was part of school regulations. My mother then went to the school board of Philadelphia and asked for the food. I do not know what she said, or to whom she said it, but the people at the school board fell in love with her, and her wish was their command. They told her she could take the food to the needy families. They subsequently offered her a job within the school system. My father was not really happy about this because he was accustomed to my mother being barefoot and pregnant but he knew those days were over. He agreed to let her work part-time only. My mother started working for the school board and at my school as a teacher's aide, and she just loved it. When we got older, or should I say, when the youngest child, my sister Michelle started school, my mother's career took off. My mother's encounter with the school board officials and the community went to another level. And yes, she still kept her daily task of taking food from the school to give to needy families.

After helping so many people in the community with jobs, food, traffic tickets, clothing, and being released from jail, she became one of the most powerful women in Philadelphia. My mother was now a success, and some described her as an overnight wonder. Before she knew it, the mayor and other city officials were coming to her for help with minority votes. People who wanted to run for office would come to my mother first, so she would endorse them. If they were credible and were really going to help African Americans and poor people, she would do it. Everyone she backed won. She put many Philadelphia officials in office, and some are still there today.

Often, my mother would call us at home in the middle of the week and say, "Put on your Church clothes. Your daddy is coming to get you." She meant all eight of us Coleys who were living in the family home. We were going to the "victory" parties of the political officials. At the time, we had no idea what was going on. We only knew that the hotel banquet rooms were very beautiful, especially the table settings. Many political people would come over to our table and say they had never seen such a large group of children who were so well-mannered. My parents always got compliments like that about us. We carried our last name well, even today, thank you Jesus! My mother always had my daddy right there and made sure it was clear to everyone who he was. I never, in all the days of my life with my parents, heard my mother say anything negative about my daddy. *Never!!!*

Although, my mother was very successful politically with helping people vote and register to vote along with other community support, this was not her first encounter with helping people. While we were young, my mother was asked by our pastor, Reverend Leon H. Sullivan of Zion Baptist Church to help him lead the Tasty Kake march in the early sixties. Tasty Kake, one of the oldest snack food factories in the United States was based in Philadelphia, was not hiring African Americans during that time. This march turned out to be a success, and it helped many African-Americans to obtain jobs. It also paved the way for people today in other aspects of employment in terms of helping them stand up for equality.

My mother did several things like this, but not too many, because her family always, always came first. I am so proud to know how she has helped so many people make it in life.

I am so very proud to have my mother's name, because she truly left me a legacy. I am even more fortunate to have my parental grandmother's first name as my middle name on my father's side. So, my mother's name was Lillie Charlene Coley and my name is Lillie Marie Coley. But, more importantly, I am glad I have my father's last name. I am a true Coley.

I am happy that my mother was the first woman I ever knew during my childhood. Being the first real female image in my life, she set the pace, or tone, for me as I grew older. This is why it is so important that she lived this thing called life the very best she could. This was imperative because all of her children were watching every move she made. I looked up to her because I knew one day I would be like her, or at least that's what I thought as a child. Fortunately, I became a lot like her. I am so glad she set such a beautiful example for me to follow. It is hard to tell somebody to live something that you are not living yourself.

Now, we know everybody makes mistakes and falls short, but we must learn to get over that. I want to know: are you trying to live this thing called life right, or, are you just pretending?

James O. Coley, Sr.
(Photo Does Not Display His Real Skin Tone)

Chapter 4

The First Man I Ever Loved:
My Father

ere's my daddy. My father had a white father and a half-white mother with green eyes. This picture of my father does not show his true complexion. For those who know him knew he was very fair-skinned. I needed to mention this for clarity since many of his friends and family did not recognize him in this picture, but this was all that I had. It's very interesting to think about your father and the part he plays in your life. It is so crucial for children to be raised by both parents and to have a father who takes an active role in defining and shaping their lives. For me, my daddy was everything, and I know I was a daddy's little girl.

He loved all his girls. My dad took special—pride in being sensitive toward us. He never—not one time raised his voice or hand to any of his girls. He always left the discipline of us to our mother.

My father was very mild-mannered. Although he appeared to some to be big and strong, he was really a sensitive person. He was from a large family in Goldsboro, North Carolina, and he was the baby. Daddy's family was financially secure, and this was why we had an economically stable family. He was definitely taken care of because he was the baby. People down South believe in family.

My father said that his father always beat him, and this was probably why he never really wanted to hit his children, especially his daughters. He was extremely close to his mother, mainly because of the abuse from his father. It was in his mother's arms where he found safety and comfort. When his mother died of natural causes during his late thirties, he never recovered from her death. He became engrossed in his work until he met my mother then he clung to her the same way he had to his mother. My father's behavior was very addictive or compulsive in that he took everything he believed in seriously, sometimes too seriously. I think I am like that, too, but I am more balanced and I try to use wisdom mixed with common sense to combat compulsive behavior. Some of his behavior stemmed from childhood pain that was never healed.

My father was very old-fashioned and believed the man should be the provider and builder of the house. He was our sole provider for a long time. He did allow my mother to work, as mentioned earlier, but not until after my youngest sister, Michelle, started school. He was a good man and definitely a family man who would do whatever was asked of him (well almost). He liked taking us to the park, to parades, and to carnivals. He really enjoyed his children; we were always out doing something. My mother enjoyed taking us to the movies.

In addition to swimming daddy taught all of us how to skate, ride bikes, ride a horse/pony, fish, camp, and so many other activities. I really loved and appreciated him because he participated in the activities with us when he could. Mommie usually stayed home while we were out with our daddy. This gave her time to take care of the house and time for herself. I don't ever remember being bored at home in the haven my dad had created, or with our outdoor activities. Daddy liked the outdoors and Mommie liked the house.

At one of our outdoor activities, a parade, I remember wandering off and getting lost. I was scared because I could not find my daddy, my brothers, or my sisters. Finally, Daddy saw me from a distance and yelled, "Marie!" with concern in his voice. I really felt something when he called me, remembering that Marie was his mother's name. I ran to him crying, and I thought he was going to be mad at me but he gently stroked me on my back and said, "Don't worry, Daddy's here." I felt safe again.

A father is truly the first man a little girl should know and when he is good to her, she adores him. She knows that she is not his gender, but he is somewhere inside of her and vice versa. It is through her relationship with her father that a girl knows she is special, and when she grows up to become a woman, she is able to make better choices in male relationships. My father always said, "Don't marry anybody unless they are like me," and I would say, "Okay, Daddy. I won't."

My father loved to travel, and we had an orange station wagon to take us anywhere we wanted to go as a family. Daddy took us to many different states for sightseeing and eating. We traveled down South to see his family often.

My daddy loved his brothers and sisters, and they thought that he was gold. Of course, they were right. Daddy came from a line of preachers, so there is no wonder that I was called to the ministry, too. Our family knew all our cousins, aunts, and uncles of both my parents. We did not suffer the loss of not knowing who our family was. Dad's family did not visit much because most of them were older, but many are still living today. My mother's family came to our home each year for Thanksgiving and Christmas. It was mostly my mother's family who attended, since they lived in Philadelphia. My mother was the administrator for the family. She kept everybody together. Holidays were the most precious time of the year, and my parents made sure we were happy. My birthday is right after Christmas but my parents never cheated me of a gift. They always had something extra set aside for me.

Daddy didn't say much to people. He just observed. My mother was just the opposite. She was more outgoing. It is really ironic because I believe I look like both my parents and act like both of them. I always tell people I am split down the middle. My father came from a family with knowledge about finance. My mother came from a family with knowledge of math and science. This explains why all my brothers and sisters are knowledgeable either in math, science, or both. Also, we have a spirit of prosperity that allows us to generate, make, and sense or smell money.

I must confess that when I was a child, I thought that my father was a god. I knew that there was a God up above and over everyone, but I also thought everybody's family had a little god, their father basically, someone who protects the family. I think around the age of seven, I found out there is only one true God.

I believe, with all that's within me, that my father, who was truly the first man I ever loved, and then my brothers to follow, set the tone for how I would be expected to be treated by men once I got older. My father never used foul language toward us or raised his voice. He was very gentle and patient when we were growing up. He was truly my covering, and I felt safe because of him. I thank God today for my dad, because he has a place in my heart that no man can take. Often, women who do not have a good relationship with their father tend to seek it in other relationships with men. Women who never experience this love early often accept men who are very abusive and disrespectful. I cannot even imagine taking anything but God's best.

I love my father immensely and am so glad that I encountered such a meaningful relationship with him. This foundation will be with me for the rest of my life.

Chapter 5

Our Family—A Bond That Can Never Be Broken

One of the most powerful tools that my mother used to keep us connected while we were growing up was communication. Truly, that was one of her gifts. She believed in talking about our issues, to hear and to understand our opinions and views.

Each of my brothers and sisters is unique and special. We were obedient children who believed everything that our parents told us. We never questioned anything unless we did not understand. If my mother said the sky was purple, we would have believed it even though it looked blue. My family often had round-table discussions about family issues. I remember one time my parents had to take care of some business affairs and were gone pretty much the whole day. That day my brother James whom we called Odell decided that he would hit us girls. I guess he was just in a bad mood. While he was hitting us and chasing us around the house, he said, "And you better not tell Mommy and Daddy or next time I will hit you harder." He was trying to scare us so we would not tell them.

My parents came home that evening and we had dinner. Talk about a mother's instinct. My mother could tell something was wrong. Of course, brothers and sisters hit and fight all the time, but it should not be excessive. After dinner my mother said that we were going to have a family talk, and so we did. Odell looked at me very sternly. The look meant, "You better not say anything." He knew I was outspoken and would probaly say something. My parents went around the table to each child and asked questions. When they got to me, I told them exactly what happened. My mother looked into my brother's eyes and said firmly and with authority, "Don't you *ever* put your hands on your sisters again," and she told me to let her know if he did. My brother never laid a hand on any of us again. Odell was close to my age and did not really hurt me, but it was the principle of hitting his sisters that mattered. If he had gotten away with it, he might have grown up thinking it was okay to hit women. Since Daddy made our house our haven, we had to get along. If my parents had to take care of business, they wanted to be assured we were safe in the house.

I believe through these different types of experiences and family discussions, my siblings and me grew closer through love and respect for one another. My brothers today respect all of their sisters in the same way they did when the foundation was laid many years ago.

My brother Andrew was my mother's first child from her first marriage. He was a very caring and sensitive person who did not talk much, but when he did, he had a lot to say. Unfortunately, he is no longer with us. He died in 1979 at the age of thirty-nine, possibly from poison. We are not sure what happened, even today.

Frank, my second oldest brother, loves music, can bake the best cake you have ever tasted, and is an electronics genius. He is the family lawyer; he is the one who has helped to keep law and order in the family. Over the years, Frank has always been there to support his family, no matter what.

Edwina is the third child. Edwina can also cook, and she is considered the queen bee of the family because she is always giving advice.

Edward, our other brother, has always been quiet, sweet, and mysterious. I always thought he would be a priest, but he got married and is a Philadelphia police officer. Eddie is very loving and sensitive person and, I believe he always will be.

My sister Shirl is the first Coley from my parents' marriage. Shirl was going to be our first family doctor— gynecologist, and then veterinarian. Unfortunately, she injured her hand on her computer job and could not pursue her education. Shirl was a good student at Penn State University. She also kept the family together when we were young and still does.

My brother James, also known as Odell, is named after our daddy. He has always been the "man with the plan." Odell was very popular and won several awards in high school from best looking to best dressed. The average guy hated him because all the girls loved him. Odell believes in family and loves to see us come together. He is involved in electronics but mostly in telecommunication. He is extremely intelligent and speaks very well. I believe he has been called into the ministry to preach God's word, but he is not sure yet.

Next is Joseph. He is almost exactly like my father. Joe is very, very smart. He has been saving his money and investing in the stock market since he was about fifteen years old. He reads a lot and loves to talk with family and friends.

Kurt is sensitive and sweet. Many women would love to have him, but they must go through his sisters. We love him dearly; he is the baby boy.

I would be next in line, but I'll tell you about me later.

The twins come after me: Yvette and Annette are fraternal twins who are both unique and special. Yvette is a premed student and works as a criminal justice professional, and my sister Annette manages several Marriott Hotels.

Last, but not least, is my sister Michelle. Michelle was going to be our next doctor, but this was not completed due to some personal circumstances. Michelle, too, is very intelligent and has great potential and a wonderful future ahead of her.

Although families can have physical bonds, the main objective for all families should be spiritual bonds that are strengthened by praying together. God has truly been good to us. He has allowed us to have a bond that no one can break. One thing about us: we don't allow anyone to talk about another member or to harm us. We protect each protect one another's integrity. My family up until this point for the most part has made good, wise, and moral decisions over the years. None of my brothers have been to jail and none of us have been in the divorce courts. We have pretty much had a stable life. Praise the Lord!

Chapter 6

Unresolved Issues

When issues or circumstances go unattended or are not dealt with, they often become bigger and more complex than we are. Because I have been a Christian most of my life, it has always been important for me to understand my weaknesses and faults so I could ask God to give me strength to overcome my problems. The devil wants us to leave things unresolved in the hopes that he can one day use them against us.

My mother become very powerful in the city of Philadelphia in the mid-seventies. Initially, my father did not have a problem with my mom's political work. My father, who always played the role of provider, basically controlled the entire household.

There were many types of men and women who came to our house frequently, especially during political campaign time. My mother kept us out of sight while she was home taking care of her political business. She did not want us visible to people she really did not know. Daddy was there most of the time when he was not working.

My mother had several city officials, all of whom were men with keys to the city, coming to our home. They thought very highly of my mother and really thought she was the best thing since sliced bread. They were right! My father became insecure about this, but my mother made sure he was comfortable with the visitors. She was able to relieve some of my dad's insecurities for a while, but they really began to overtake him. His insecurities or weaknesses were just waiting for the right moment to appear and take control. Negative things inside of us, which are not resolved by God's love and power, can and will come to the surface in the right circumstances. It is only by the grace of God that certain things do not surface that could be detrimental. We must have God's love and His power to handle circumstances that overwhelm us, otherwise it could cost us something we may not be willing to pay.

While Daddy was in the Marines for twenty-five years, he was an electrician and often did some cooking. He was a part of the Marine Corp that went out to sea periodically. My father knew how to do all kinds of electrical work. Today, people with this skill are called electrical engineers. He learned this in the service. My father was also in finance. He was good with money and investments. Unfortunately, Daddy was obsessed with money. Because his family had it and he was successful, money became his god. That was all he would talk about—money, money, money. He once told me that you didn't have to go to Church if you had money, and I just looked at him like he was crazy because I knew that was not right. Ironically, he would go to Church with us anytime we asked but we need a relationship with God, not religion.

Daddy was obsessed with money, my mother, and his children, in that order. He built his life around these three areas. He felt that he owned us because he loved us, provided for us, and watched over us. He had been taught by his family values that a man has possession of his wife and family. But, his possession turned into an obsession. You could not tell he had this problem. Often it takes specific circumstances to trigger a reaction to unresolved issues. This is why it is essential to solve problems when they occur, because the devil will make sure that your area of weakness comes back to haunt you. He will manipulate you into a situation to challenge your weakness so you will break under pressure. When we have God in our lives like we should, when we become weak, He will help us be strong. He also strengthens us to fight against the adversary. But, if we are not covered by God's power, we're fighting the devil almost by ourselves. The devil has a lot of power, but God has *all* power. Life's not designed for you to make it by yourself. Everybody needs help.

Since my mother was visible as the people who won the election, head officials of the city such as the mayor asked her to run for state representative. They were sure she would win due to her track record and relationship with the community. My parents talked about it, and my father decided that he would support her. Later he changed his mind. That was when my parents started to have serious problems.

Daddy was very intimidated and insecure because some of the men with whom my mother worked had more money and power than he did. He started to see that he was losing control. He knew my mother was going to win the political office and would become more powerful than he was but he was more concerned with losing her to these other powerful men who had the keys to the city.

During my mother's campaign for state representative in 1976, Daddy had to see people constantly come in and out of our house. Then the real test came. My mother was advised that she and her family needed to move to the suburbs before she appeared on the ballot because it would be too dangerous for us children to live in the heart of the city. She agreed and told my dad. He disagreed because he could not see other people telling him where he should live, and he rebelled. At that point, my mother was so close to being on the ballot and the actual day of election was so near that she moved on with her plans without telling my father everything. My mother was arranging for us to move to upstate New York where my brother Andrew lived. She had planned to keep her Philadelphia residency but wanted her children far away from the city. My parents began to argue about this, and that was the first time my siblings and me heard them argue. Of course, I know now, as an adult, that they must have had other arguments, but we had never heard or seen them. In the past, they must have waited for us to go bed to discuss sensitive issues.

Daddy went back and forth about his decision to support my mother's potential political career. He was very unstable, about his decision to support her, and of course, this began to frustrate my mother. I mentioned previously that my daddy really loved his mother and was very, very close to her. He clung to her when she died, and he *never* recovered normally from her death. Oftentimes, people become too close to others which can create unhealthy relationships. There should always be balance in life, especially when dealing with others. People are so fickle and unstable. We sometimes put too much faith in others who are struggling themselves. Having healthy expectations and realistic goals gives people room to be themselves and grow into where they are going. If someone dies, we should be able to function mentally, physically, and financially without them. We will miss our loved ones and are entitled to a grieving period, but we must have the strength to move on in life. Well, my father had his family, but, of course, no one can really take the place of your momma. He suppressed the loss of his mother along with his childhood pain. When issues are suppressed and not resolved up front, they surface later in life in ways one would never, ever expect. Be a problem solver. Learn to look at your situation clearly and objectively, and deal with it and all the pain that goes with it. Remember, attitude determines your altitude. How you view and handle problems determines how high you will go in life. Life's outcome is ten percent what happens to you and ninety percent how you react to what happens to you. Even in your daily life, learn not to react to people in negative ways, because in doing so, you tell on yourself. Seek to find the strength to overcome and become a victor instead of a victim.

When my mother came into my father's life during the 1950s, he clung to her the way he had to his mother. Depending on someone so much that you cannot function was neither normal nor healthy behavior. Every tub should be able to stand on its on bottom. Now I know that my mother was designed and destined to help my father help himself, for that is what relationships are all about. None of us can or will reach perfection, but there should be some progress in our behavior. The problem with my parents' marriage was that my father brought his baggage into the relationship. This is not to say we don't all bring baggage, but it was the size of the baggage that made the difference. He had a very large, unresolved issue. His pain from childhood abuse hurt him to the core. It was unbearable for him to think about it and to face.

Unbearable pain, I must say, should be handled with care. Mothers in our society—if they really love their sons and even their daughters—should not let their children become so attached that they cannot make it in society after they are gone. Having suppressed problems and unresolved issues can lead to abnormal behavior. My father felt, and was probably taught, that he could get by and make it with his money, so he went through life thinking money was really all he needed to be truly happy. Of course, after he had my mother and his children, he really had what some would have considered the perfect life. But somehow, when Mommie ran for political office, he thought he was losing all that he had worked so hard to build. It must have seemed like building a house from the ground up then having someone come along and either take it before you got to move in, or throwing you out after you had really lived there.

My parents were not seeing eye to eye about my mother's political career, and my father decided he had to take matters in his own hands. He was not going to lose the woman to whom he had devoted his whole life—the woman he provided for, protected, cared for, and loved. After all, he felt no other man did what he did for her, so he felt he owned her and us. The bottom line was, he could not stand the thought of losing someone else he loved so much again. So, because my daddy was obsessed with my mother and could not dream of living without her, he decided to take her life and his. Yes, my parents left this life through murder-suicide when I was eleven years old. My father took his life and my mother's on February 20, 1977, the day before my mother was going on the ballot to run for state representative, because he felt time was running out. My mother was forty-six years of age and my father was fifty-two. All eight children from my parents' marriage were living in the house at the time, and our ages ranged from seven to sixteen. Michelle, the youngest, was seven years old, and my sister, Shirl, the oldest, was sixteen years old.

My father committed the tragic acts while we were asleep, but we awoke when we heard turmoil. So, we saw and heard it all. The house went into chaos. We were all over the house in a panic. Need I say more? It was truly a mess and a shock for us children to see the man we loved and adored do such a thing.

My father was crying when the ambulance took him out on the stretcher, and he was asking for forgiveness and repeatedly saying, "I did not mean to do it, I did not mean to do it." My mother died almost instantly, and Daddy died when he arrived at the hospital. My father used a knife to take his own life as well. All this violence took place in our family home.

My siblings and I were in a state of shock and pain. I personally was devastated and could not stop crying, especially when I saw my father taken out on a stretcher. When he saw me he broke down and cried even harder. We both shared a bond that was unbreakable. He often told me how I looked like and acted like his mother. I loved this man so, so much. When we were told both our parents were dead, my siblings and I all went into the basement, our haven, and cried and embraced one another. I think more than anything we had experienced the shock of our lives.

My family heard rumors and really believed that someone called my father anonymously, someone who may have been an opponent of my mother's in the race, and told him some unpleasant things about Mother and other men. It was no secret that most of the men liked her because she was every man's dream. But we never thought anyone would be evil enough to call my father. These people knew my father's weakness and used it against him. Well, there's one thing about politics: it sometimes can be a dirty game that can become deadly. My father always said that if he could not have my mother, nobody would.

Typically speaking, some people love hard and are very serious when it comes to relationships with the opposite sex. But we all must be careful that this love does not go too far and turn into obsession, which is an unhealthy form of love that has turned into a sickness. A person who is obsessed believes he cannot function properly without another person. He has become so emotionally dependent that his thinking and behavior become abnormal and distorted as it relates to this individual. It usually takes something negative to trigger this chemical imbalance, and once it happens, the person goes into a state of temporary insanity.

In a nutshell, a person who is obsessed has a void in his life that the object of his affection has been able to be touch, but God can touch it better. It is unhealthy to depend on someone so much that you are willing to hurt others. This is not a win-win situation. You both lose if someone gets hurt.

With Daddy not wanting my mother to run for office, with his children moving to another state, and with someone calling him to spread rumors about my mother, he went temporarily insane. And, no, he was not always like that. I know because I lived with him. His behavior was triggered by unresolved issues that had been suppressed for years and never dealt with. He tried to handle them by obtaining money, a beautiful wife, a big house, a big car, and wonderful children, but something on the inside of him was crying out for help.

When you make anything your god—whether it is a person, place, or a thing—God will let it destroy you eventually unless you seek Him for help and direction. Many of us have unresolved issues that God is constantly dealing with us about. We must let Him take us through the process to freedom. It takes certain circumstances to trigger negative things inside of us that may have been lying dormant. Setting up the circumstances or traps, ladies and gentlemen, is one of the oldest tricks of the enemy.

The devil knows what will make us "go off," especially if we are not a Christian or not a mature Christian. God specializes in taking our weaknesses and turning them into successes, which is why Paul says in the scripture, "When I am weak, He is strong." This applies to believers, those who have accepted Christ as their personal savior. I do not know if my father was a "believer," and he did not appear to have been raised with strong Christian values. He did have values, but they were not strong or Christian-based. All I know is that he was a good man who loved his family and took very, very good care of us. But how many of us know that is not enough—I see you raising your hands—you must be "born again," washed by the blood of Jesus. But, what the devil meant for evil, God meant for good. You will see in later chapters how God changed tragedy into an opportunity.

So much for my fairy-tale childhood. God was the first one who told me that my siblings and I had a "fairy-tale childhood that ended in a tragedy," but my question was, "Why us?" Now you see why God helped me to retain my childhood memories and why He allowed us to have such good times together. He knew it was going to end early. So, many people knew about the tragedy in our hometown because it was something you would not forget and because our family was very much in the limelight. We were constantly in the public's eye, years before this tragedy.

It is important for me to paint the whole picture. Many times people only know half the story, or just the bad part. Well, my brothers and sisters and I had more good memories with our parents than bad. One person I knew kept begging me to tell her about how my parents died. She had the nerve to ask me and I told her. So, again for clarity, and because she tried to change my story after I told it to her, let this record show and tell the way it really was. My father did use a knife, not a gun. I had told this person who was supposed to be a Christian specifically that my father used a knife. She tried to change the story by telling other people that it was a gun.

People always want to know your business, then misquote you on purpose when they tell others. These people have a lot to hide, and believe me, this person had more problems/secrets than anybody I knew. So, whenever you hear something, especially from a Church busybody, consider the source and know that these people are mentally ill and in denial of the many horrible problems that are happening in their own lives. People changing others' words can cause so much pain and make some not want to tell their story. Be brave and share your tale anyway because someone may need to hear it and become healed.

After my parents' death, my sister Edwina, brother Frank and my mother's sister, Annie, helped raise us.

I know, and the rest of my brothers and sisters know, that my father did not mean to take my mother's life. We forgave him instantly, but the hurt and loss were still there so deep it was indescribable. How were we going to live without two people we absolutely adored? We never, not once, made an excuse for our father. We said he was dead wrong for what he did. But understanding what obsession means and knowing how he was raised helps my siblings and me to live with what happened better. So, I know first-hand what unresolved issues can do to a family.

My dad needed to have God's influence in his life so he would not depend on people to give him what only God can supply. We all have a void that is left in us on purpose by God that only, only God Himself can fill. Whatever we need, God's got it.

Even with all that happened, even when our beloved father caused so much pain to come into our lives, the love he showed us and the love God gave us provided us the power to forgive him. It takes power to forgive when the pain of hurt aches every part of your body. And, to this day, I will not let anyone talk badly about my daddy. Even now I have my head up and my arms folded, with a slight attitude if someone says something negative. Before you say something about him, please look at yourself first and the mistakes you have made. Now that you have remembered, see how people had to forgive you. Well, that's the same way we forgave our father. There is no such thing as big sins and little sins; it is just the consequences of certain sins that are different. My father's sin cost his life and my mother's. For those of us who are living, there are no more excuses. We all need to be doing better.

Having said all that, *I still won't let anybody talk about my daddy.* Thank you very much. And, as I stated before, we never heard my mother say one negative thing about our father. Not one thing.

Masking a problem does nothing but allow it to overtake you later in life. It is the design of the devil to let you suppress and not address the issue. He wants your problem to wipe you out one day. Communication is the best tool we have in solving issues. We should use it wisely. One thing about me, I will never get ulcers because I worry about nothing. I speak my mind as diplomatically as I can about issues and concerns. Once I've said it, I am done with it. I do not keep going over it. My godparents always taught me "not to nurse it or rehearse it." Once you have said your peace, stop talking about it, and disperse it to God. If you keep talking about it, just brings up old feelings. Learn to forgive through love, which conquers all things. Ask God to teach you how to love. Everyone must be taught about this tool, since we generally come into the world as selfish beings until we learn otherwise. God will teach you what love is and what love is not.

In "Lesson for Living, Part, 1" page 137 in the back of this book, there is some very good information on gaining and maintaining wealth God's way. We do not need to be lovers of money. But we should be friends with money. Jesus talks about being friends with money in the Book of Corinthians. This means that when you get paid on Friday, you still have some money left on Monday.

Learn to save and invest and not put your money in "things" or material possessions only. God once spoke to me about this and said, "Make more and spend less." This wisdom has helped me a great deal. Understand that spending money is different than giving money. Spending subtracts or lessens your money and giving multiplies your money and other areas of your life.

Chapter 7

Silence Broken After 10 Years
The Beginning of Mending
a Broken Heart

My immediate family and I, that is, the eight Coleys living in my parents' home, after the initial counseling did not talk about our tragedy for ten years after it occurred. As a matter of fact we pretended it had not happened and that our parents were on vacation and would be returning home soon. It was my brother Odell who forced us to face reality one day. "We have to stop pretending that Mommie and Daddy are still here. They are dead. They are dead," he said firmly. After he spoke, reality started to set in. God used him to ignite something inside of us to make us confront our pain and discouragement. Silence is part of the enemy's trap. You cannot be healed from something until it is exposed correctly. Breaking our silence was the first step to confronting our pain and anger.

During our mending process, God put our hearts back together one day at a time and one piece at a time. If your heart needs healing first, you must admit the problem has literally crushed your soul. Then, you must seek to get the ultimate healing. No food, job, sexual experience, money, or person can fix a problem like God can. Pretending something has not happened, as we know, is a form of denial, which is an early stage of mental illness.

Most people think those who are in mental institutions just woke up crazy, but that's not so. These people had situations and problems that they could not deal with in their own minds. Yes, some will walk around all their lives living a lie, knowing that they are hiding the truth.

The truth can be so buried within them that they start believing the lie. Their minds turn into a reprobate one, which causes them to make excuses for everything, even when you know biblically, financially, morally, and socially that it is not right. There are many people who have been abused, not just verbally or physically, but mentally. They will continue to ignore the truth about themselves, their children, and their spouses. No problem will ever be resolved fully and completely unless people get free from it. Isolation causes frustration. No man is an island unto himself. Life has been designed so that we may help and encourage one another.

It is always best to expose the enemy in your own life before someone else does. Often, when people find out something negative about you, they cannot wait to tell someone else. This is why I am telling my story, because nobody can tell it like I can tell it. When we tell, we are healed faster. Of course, we must always use wisdom and common sense.

Ask God to give you clarity of thought and articulation of speech about what to say and not to say. But the healing process requires that you release that which hurts you in some constructive way. Communication is the best way because it is so therapeutic. As you release the negative in a healthy way, then you have room to fill yourself up with positive things. "From the abundance of the heart the mouth speaketh." (Matthew 12:34, KJV)

Whether it is financial debt or spiritual lack, one must, and I say must, confess their mess, look it straight in the face, and say, "I've had enough." If it is financial, it is all right to tell people that you do not have the money because you have debt to clear up. And, it's all right to tell people if your spouse is not faithful. Learn to tell the truth and shame the devil.

I had to be honest with myself first about my parents' death, and then I took it to the Lord in prayer. There is one thing about God that I just absolutely love: He is a good listener. And, for those of you who do not know, I love to talk. Sometimes I do keep quiet, mostly when I am asleep. Even then, I am talking, but mostly in my spiritual language or "tongues." Someone knows what I mean out there. I must confess that God has helped me a great deal with my tongue. I still have some ways to go, but I am not going to be a silent Mother Teresa; that is not coming.

I know some people say they have made it quite nicely without God, but if the truth be told, I'm gonna tell it. The Bible says that the sun shines on the just and the unjust. This is why unbelievers get by, but not for long.

God's mercy truly does abound within our hearts and minds. God was so precious toward my family that it was almost unbelievable. He let each and every one of us release our anger about our parents' tragedy the best way we knew how. But we were still covered by the blood of Jesus. All of us, from one year to the next, released the anger upon the earth. Then God moved in, covered, and mended our wounded hearts, and led us into another stage of growth and development. He taught and brought us from a mighty long way. The heart is the place where we rationalize our emotions, and the mind is where we reason why we should do something. If the heart and mind are of one accord, then the body follows.

Brokenness often stems from pain and lack of understanding. Once more data or information is received through revelation knowledge, and life's untimely circumstances, it is then that we can reach another level of growth.

Our childhood tragedy broke my siblings and me into emotional pieces of hurt. Once the hurt took place, then the reasoning kicked in. But through love and being open-minded, our hearts were changed.

Rahab, a harlot in the Bible, seized the opportunity to change. She did not make excuses about why she was doing what she was doing but when given the chance, her heart and mind were in touch with each other. We all know that before a person has a great fall, something happened to get them there. Often, it is pride, ego, or shame. Pride definitely goeth before a fall. Not being able to say "I am sorry," "I made a mistake," or "I love you" can destroy any type of relationship. It takes a mature person to admit his mistakes and to have a spirit of reconciliation.

Some people are afraid to change because they are worried about what others think. We must be delivered from people and their opinions in order to really be set free.

One thing about me is that I do not fear anyone but God. I will respect and revere my husband once I am covered through marriage, but nobody can move me but God. From a really young age, I never cared about what negative people thought or said because what they think really does not matter. Until people are able to wake me up in the morning, pump warm blood in my veins, and speak to my spirit, I really don't care what they think.

After breaking the silence the more my siblings and I talked about our parents' tragedy, the better the pain of loss seemed to get. I realized that every time I spoke about their death I felt a burden being lifted. I then discovered after reflecting on my life how my mother taught all us kids the power of communication. Each time I spoke to people about them being dead, I was actually ministering to myself. One of the greatest lessons I learned from my mother was how to share what I was feeling. The things I miss the most about my parents is their cooking, bear hugs, and their presence. I just loved being around them both. After breaking our silence my siblings and I started to live a more normal life. We took one day at a time while trying to cope with our loss. During the midst of our storm we learned to build one another up while seeking God for strength. God never failed us but kept us every step of the way. The devil wanted to shame us by keeping us silent about what, how, and when it happened. But, my siblings and I had nothing of which to be ashamed because we came from good cloth, both spiritually and physically. It was a good thing that went bad.

Chapter 8

Our Parents Set The Foundation
They Left Us A Legacy

Foundations are very important in life. This is usually what an individual will use as a basis for achievements. It was with these tools that I am able to write this book today. God has truly, truly been merciful to me, and I would never take the credit from Him. And, I know He definitely has all power and is all knowing. But even God gives us all free will to make our own decisions. In order to make the right decision, the proper seeds or information must be planted within the individual. I believe, with all that is in me, that my parents set the pace for my life in making decisions. They taught values, love, and togetherness, but,

59

most of all, they taught morals and knowing right from wrong. These were the main legacies they left us.

When raising children, it is imperative that they learn the ability to call wrong wrong and right right. This concept of morals mixed with Christianity develops a well-defined consciousness. This is why it's important for young men and women who are reading this book to make sure they do their very best to be examples of goodness to their children and the children in their community.

Our lives, especially when we are young, are greatly impacted by what we see other people do that it is indescribable. Many adults who are grown today have been taught wrong as a child, and now they are acting it out. The frightening thing is, many don't see it. Others who do not know God may not see Him revealing it to them. This kind of person is not really living a free life, and as a result, there are broken communities full of people who are carrying a lot of baggage from their childhood. My siblings and I lived in a very controlled environment, and although there should be some balance in this, every child needs to understand and relate to boundaries. I do not know where any of us would be if we did not have someone actually living this thing called life.

Speaking of having a good foundation, a male detective tried to make a move on my sister on the same day of our tragedy just a few hours after the incident in *our house*. Can you believe this? He saw this beautiful sixteen year-old virgin who was the oldest in our home. Forget the detective, it was the devil trying to come in to destroy us. He had accomplished getting my parents, but this was not enough; he also wanted us kids.

My sister might have felt vulnerable and let the detective woo her into his arms if not for my parents' foundation. It is typical for young girls to feel that an older man, especially during a tragic time would be there for support and not for his own personal gain. He was tempted by our immaculate home and this young girl. My parents were not even in the grave yet, and the devil was after us. This is why it is so important to set a foundation for your children, so when they are approached in a negative way, they can handle it.

After this incident, my brothers basically protected us girls from male friends. Any male who wanted to talk to us had to go through our brothers, and we were always chaperoned by them until we got older. I hated the way they criticized our male friends, but now I'm so glad they did.

God used my brothers to protect their sisters' bodies and reputations. The enemy thought he had us, but as stated, God let him take two, but he could not touch the eight. We were covered with the blood of Jesus. (I'm shouting right about now.)

Chapter 9

Remembering The Way We Were:
This Keeps Our Parents Alive
In Our Hearts

I believe the best way to keep people alive is to talk about them and reflect on their memories. Memories are reflected encounters of life that have taught us and brought us to where we are. In other words, we are the sum of our past, which has been designed to help us grow into our future. As you reflect and understand where you have been, it is then and only then that you can go to the next level in life. People have a tendency not to want to think about the past because it often brings up so much hurt. But God often wants us to face our accuser, and it is through these encounters that healing can take place. We can be healed in the very place of our pain. Ask me. I know!

My family and I had to understand what happened, come to terms with it, forgive, and move on. I can honestly say that we have more good than bad memories of our parents. But understanding obsession helped us to better accept why this tragedy took place. As children we did not even know how to spell the word obsession, let alone what it meant. But over the years, by God's grace, we have all overcome.

I look at healing as living water. It never touches one person or one place, but, just like water, when it spills, it touches all that is around it. Now, living water will ignite what it touches, and bringing life to anything that needs it. It is imperative that we all learn lessons in life, because, otherwise, we may find ourselves falling into the same behavior patterns. Lessons in life teach us about ourselves and lead us on a road to recovery. The places where it leads us often help us to apply what we have learned during our pain and healing to help others who are going through similar situations. This is what true destiny and purpose in life is all about: helping others to help themselves.

It is important to remember that hurting people hurt people. Whole people help heal people and make them become stronger. While we are getting life lessons, they are never just for us but for others who will come behind us and alongside us.

We cannot become something or somebody until we first come to God. This must be our self-will. Once we "come" then we "become" what God has intended for us to be. Once you become what you need to be, then you have something to offer or bring to the table. You then provide and enhance a healthier relationship and outlook with others. I always tell the ladies in my empowerment workshops they need to "be" what they are looking for in a mate. Some have very high expectations for the man they want in their lives but have accomplished very little within themselves. You need to be what you are looking for, or something close to it. This analogy also applies in other areas of life, such as careers.

Attitude determines altitude. How you react to things and people tells a lot about you. This also lets the devil know what type of traps and bones to put out for you. Learn to "chill," and remember you must pick your battles. Every war is not worth fighting. You need wisdom and spiritual discernment. If my siblings and me had reacted to the shock of our parents' death by being unforgiving and with other types of negative reactions, we would not have made it here today. Life would have eaten us up. Holding grudges will destroy you. Forgiveness, however, frees you to live, grow, and move on.

Learning to forgive at an early age prepares you for the hurts that will come later in life. My family had to put something in our hearts called love in order to receive the reward of being free in our spirits. No deposit, no return; what you put out is what you get back. Little in, little out; Little praise, little results; big praise, big results. I am a living witness this is true.

Life truly is the best teacher. Also, watching other people with their successes and failures has helped me to avoid pitfalls and unnecessary problems. I am truly a preventive maintenance person. If I can prevent something before it happens, I will. I do take some risks, provided the cost or consequence is not too great. In other words, I weigh it out and pray on it. Writing this book is a risk. I'd like to call it, the ultimate disclosure. But, when you are free from something, you can talk about it. In doing so, I know that I will be able to help others learn to share. Revealing my private family matters to the entire world is a step of faith for me. Although I have been telling my story to many, there is nothing like telling the whole world. This is the time and season to share, and I have peace in knowing this.

Chapter 10

God Said, "Two Had To Die So That Eight Could Live"

During the course of life, it is essential that one learns to forgive. This is especially important for someone like me who has been gifted with strength and stability from God. He has often guided a lot of mentally weak people to me, to whom I minister, but many of them have tried to use me, steal from me, or worry me to death. Through these experiences, however, I have learned forgiveness and the importance of it.

I was really upset with God about the whole ordeal with my parents, even after I turned twenty-five, for at this age, a lot of things were going on in my life. While growing up, I would often ask God the purpose of my parents' death, or why He allowed it to happen, even though I knew it was my father's fault. I just could not understand why God would *allow* it. "Could this have been handled a better way?" I would often ask Him and myself.

Due to my improper attitude toward God about the tragedy, as a teenager and in my early twenties, God never answered me when I asked these questions. Then one day as I was lying on my bed thinking (because I am a thinker; I can think for hours), God spoke. He said, "Two had to die so that eight could live." This revelation happened when I was twenty-five, and it came from God out of nowhere. I was not even thinking about the question or asking Him about it, but He was ready to answer.

Often, we must be in a position or posture to receive what God's got for us. If you are not ready, no matter what happens, He will not give it. I am so glad God is God, all by Himself, and He does not need any help from us. Let go and let God come into your life, so He can become your "puppet master." He desires so much for us to receive His promises, but we must be in the right frame of mind.

After God spoke this revelation into my spirit, I finally felt completion or closure to my parents' tragedy. My mind was at rest, and I had peace with this situation. In addition, my mended broken heart was now in sync with my renewed mind. They were of one accord. From this encounter, I became completely whole in this area of my life. I now felt free and had more strength to share my story with others.

God is too wise to make a mistake. If something has happened in your life that you just do not understand, turn it over to Him. He has a way of taking the worse things about our lives and turning them around to become the greatest and sweetest blessings. I will never get over my parents' death, but I have learned how to live with it better.

Chapter 11

Progeny -"Born Into The Church"

Being born into the Church is called progeny as opposed to being brought into the Church by someone, which is called proselytize. Both have advantages and disadvantages. I have often felt having a balance in life is essential to ensure success since we must learn to deal with the just and the unjust. I must admit, I was not knowledgeable about a lot of things, but God put the right people in my path who had experience with the street life. These friends helped me to handle the things I would not otherwise have known how to handle. Talk about God covering those who do not know!

I never will forget when I was in my early twenties, a friend introduced me to a gentleman who was very interested in me. I told him early that we could only be friends, and I was not looking to do anything else. He did not mind.

One day the young lady who introduced us called me and said, "Get dressed, John and Joe is coming to get us. I asked where we were going. She said, "For a ride." Well, I remembered what my brothers always said: "Wherever you go, have money for the bus to come home, just in case you get stranded," so, I took my bus pass. Both of us went in separate cars with our male friends.

My male friend, who was a nice person with creditability, seemed to be excited about our trip. I remember just riding and riding and riding until I finally asked, "Where are we going?" He said, "To a hotel!" I asked, "For what?" He said, "Well, your girlfriend called and said both of you were down (and you know for what)." I reminded him that I was not that type of woman. He said, "I know, but I thought you must have changed your mind." So, he said to me, "Well, we can still go to the hotel to watch TV and talk, since we are almost there." I said, "Are you sure you want to waste your money like that?" and he said, "It's okay." I believed him, and we went to a hotel since we were almost there. He never tried anything with me.

When I told people this story, they could not believe it. They said, "Girl, you were covered by God. Don't you know he could have raped you?" And I said, "Well, he told me he would not touch me, and I believed him." If something had happened, like if he had tried to assault me, people would not have believed my story. They would have said, "Why did you go there with him?" And, I would have said, "Because he said we would talk and watch TV."

John really did enjoy my company. More importantly, I was protected because I was covered with the blood of Jesus. He was also a respectable person, but even in an environment like that, people can become weak. It was not my intention to do anything with him because my thought pattern did not go down that street. But I cannot speak for him. When I look back at it now, it amazes me how God protected me in that situation and in every situation. (I am singing to the Lord right about now; how great Thou art.)

Often, growing up and being set apart at a young age has not been easy. People, usually my peers, who were in the Church often gave me a hard way to go because I was different. I have never professed to be better than anyone, but I know that I am not an ordinary person.

I know that God had to make me unique because He knows the end from the beginning, and He knew I was going to need all my senses to get through my parents' death. I did not have time to run the streets. I had to help keep my brothers out of jail and my sisters from getting pregnant.

I must say, I can never take all the credit for helping my siblings stay out of trouble. We all supported one another. This is why we are so close. No one person did it. God had to keep some of us more focused because we all could not be crazy at the same time.

It is important to "get saved" or become a person of faith and not become silly about life. Some of us get saved and get silly. Take the wisdom that you have learned from the streets and combine it with the morals and standards from Church to provide balance in life.

I like being a cool and together person at the same time. I am very down-to-earth and relate to all types of people on different levels. I feel I have the best of both worlds but the art of handling people is to treat everybody the same and make each person feel special.

There are risks in trying to treat everyone the same because of people's thought patterns. Some people take certain smiles and looks the wrong way. We all need good social skills, especially those of us in the public eye.

Of course, many people do not know how cool and down-to-earth I am because they don't know me. I appear on the outside to have it all together and everything just seems so perfect. Well, I do have it together, by the grace of God, but I am not perfect. I seek, like everyone else, to handle things in a mature way, but I do not achieve this goal every time.

I have had an advantage in life by starting ministry young, and this is why my work is mostly geared toward youth. However, no matter what the age, you can begin the process of living a more stable life through Jesus. As long as you have breath, you have an opportunity to grow from where you are.

Remember, Rome was not built in a day, and a baby takes nine months to develop. Do not seek fulfillment only because of what you see in others. Do it because it is just the right thing to do. It's just nice to be nice.

Life is not a race or competition with other people. It's about growing in grace and in knowledge so that you can help the people in your private and public space.

Take one day at a time and know that God will give back the time the moths ate if you have the right motives for wanting to change—to please Him and to help yourself. In doing so, you will be more useful for service to Him. That is what this is really all about. Life brings alot of changes so if you allow yourself to learn while you are growing your destiny will be more rewarding from all of life's lessons.

Chapter 12

Growing Up
Breaking Away From Family

B reaking away from my comfort zone was neither easy nor enjoyable, but in order for me to grow and to help people with my story, God needed to be able to move me around. Family is extremely important, but at some given time, we must all learn to grow up and move on. When I had to move away from my family and friends in my early twenties, God was then better able to work on me. I tell you, my greatest accomplishments have been alone. Having a lot of people around has not been part of my success story. My solitude and divine devotional time taught me the power of oneness and spiritual intimacy. During periods of times of solitude, we can reflect and reject things in our lives and people in our circle. I was never one to be around a lot of people all of the time. Although I love others, I live more for solitude. Having, or being part of, a negative clique is a poisonous and degrading experience for which I thank God I never had the appetite. Many people have wanted me to be part of their cliques. Once they saw the type of attitude I had, they were very uncomfortable around me. I was about my Father's business, which meant trying to love everybody.

I have never professed to be, and will never say I am, better than anyone else, but I know deep in my heart that I am different. Sometimes, I feel I am strange, but it is a good strange feeling. The clique I hang out with is the Trinity: God the Father, the Son and the Holy Ghost. Being a conquering woman has required me to stay focused and alert and to love myself and all those around me, so that my light can really shine and I can help others.

Chapter 13

College and Career

When I was attending college, it was hard to leave my family. I attended a university in another city but came home every weekend for family and Church. I had always dreamed of going to Howard University and did get accepted, but I did not attend because it was too far from home. After having lost my parents, it took a step-by-step process to break the cords of comfort and to give up the places of security. I will never forget the day I arrived at college. Three of my family members, Shirl, Odell, and Frank, took me to move my belongings into the dormitory and to make sure I would be okay. When they left, I almost wanted to run after the car. It was so hard to see them leave. I felt the separation. But, now it was time for me to put into practice all that I was taught. It was time for me to start to share my story more.

I am so happy to say that even during this period when I was growing up, God kept me. As "together" as I was, men were running me down. It was hard to say no but I did it. The good thing about this was that my standards for men, which were set so high by my mother when I was a girl, became a part of me. I never accepted anything less than God's best in a man, so most of the young men at college did not appeal to me.

God really helped me this way. He never let anyone unworthy come my way. One guy on campus had to have me, however. All the other girls wanted him, but he only wanted me. I considered him but quickly learned that his ego was too much for me to handle. It was the size of Kansas, and at that time in my life, the only egos I stroked were my brothers' (but in a healthy sense).

I later transferred to Temple University where I earned an undergraduate degree with a double major in computer science and math. I furthered my education in management science while studying at Eastern College and Thomas Edison College, with Thomas Edison as the awarding institution for my master's degree. Later, I went on to get a doctorate in divinity also called Theology. My studies were at Philadelphia College of Bible in Vineland, New Jersey, and International Theological Seminary (ITS), with ITS as the awarding institution. I had planned to participate in a doctorate study program at Princeton Theological Seminary, which would have supplemented my studies but did not participate due to time constraints. My last degree was completed by the age of thirty-two.

Even while I was finishing my master's, God spoke to me and said He wanted me to get my doctorate. My reply was, "I have not even finished my master's." I had intended to go back to Temple University to obtain a law degree because I wanted to become a lawyer at least part-time. I love the courtroom, along with law and order. My plan of action was changed, and once God opened the door so wide for me to receive my doctorate, I just walked in. Who would ever have thought that I would be able to receive a Ph.D.? That's why I know that if I can do it, anybody can. There were a lot of odds against me, but in spite of them, I made it through. Being obedient to God has not been easy. Doing what He has told me to do has gotten me in so much trouble, but by having faith and being steadfast, God has always come through for me. In order to obtain my blessings, my flesh (or Lillie) had to die so that my spirit woman could conquer everything God had in store for me. I was able to cross the Jordan River, a place of life or death as recorded in the Bible.

I am currently the president and founder of Community Empowerment Outreach (CEO), and I also do some work in computer engineering. CEO is a nonprofit organization that provides services to the community in job readiness; life skills, which is my passion, and other aspects of economic development. These services focus on helping youth who have gone through or who are going through traumatic circumstances. In addition, I had two community-based women's ministries called Kept Women of Jesus (KWJ) and Women of the Light (WOL).

KWJ helped others embrace and submit to God's keeping power. WOL is for women who have been called to the ministry and who need to nurture that calling. In addition, it is a network of women all over the world with whom I come in contact. I am particularly proud of both of these ministries.

These were my babies because they are the first ministries God gave me for the community.

God uses the Church as a teaching ground for believers' profound ministry and to minister to our families and those around us. Once you have gotten your training from Church, God then graduates you to the community to do real work with people who are lost and don't know Him. It's called spreading the gospel. Our Church family is where we are supposed to be nurtured, supported, and built up, so we can go out into the enemy's camp equipped and ready to fight the war.

I tell people in the Church that if you don't use your work in the community, then you are preaching to the same souls. Go out and bring new souls into the Church for God added to the Church daily.

My service in ministry started at the age of nineteen, and it escalated over the years into other stages and phases, leading me into a life of service for God.

Chapter 14

Call To Ministry Expanded

G od expanded my territory to another office of the five-fold ministry after He moved me from my home church. The five-fold ministries consist of five callings that are designed by God to serve His people and the community. These offices or positions are apostles, prophets, evangelists, pastors, and teachers, and God is your boss or CEO. I often say, "some have been called, some have been sent, and some just went." We must know in our hearts that God is, in fact, the One telling us to go forth to do His work.

God took me from the comfort zone of my home Church in Philadelphia and allowed me to go on a missionary journey in 1994 to work with another Church in a different state. Well, everything seemed okay in the beginning, but there were difficulties later. However, I truly am convinced that if you are anointed with power, God will create an atmosphere of change wherever you set your feet. And, so He did.

At this point of my ministry, I had no idea that God would call me to the other duties of ministration such as preaching. I did not even know what being called to a ministry really meant. I did realize that my first call was to teach and evangelize, but no one taught me what the five-fold ministry was really all about. After teaching youth, young adults, and adults for more than twelve years, it was not apparent what I should be. God was still fine-tuning me for my expanded calling.

After waiting on His direction, God finally spoke to me—first through others, then directly to me. He said, "Preach my word; feed my flock," and He gave me this scripture, Jeremiah 1. I said, "Was this it all this time?" He increased my territory.

After spending time with God in prayer about my new calling, He showed me I was going into the office of a preaching prophetess. I would have a prophetic voice. This is someone who sees visions about the future. After working in the Church all my life and having done everything but preach, I had no idea my call would be preaching. I was really surprised, but this explained the spiritual encounters I had while growing up. I could look back to the age of fifteen and see how God was grooming me for this position, grooming me to do Kingdom work. This also explained why I saw so many things in my life and others' lives before they happened. When I was young, I thought I was spooky because I knew things before they happened but God had started to expose me to people with the prophetic gift.

After I got clarity from God, I did what my elders told me to do. I went and told my spiritual head at the time about the revelations, but he told me that he did not believe women should be in the ministry. I was teaching adults at this Church, and he did not mind women teaching, but he did mind them preaching although preaching does not always mean from the pulpit. Whatever the case, he did not believe that women should do it. I was so hurt and crushed by the way he treated me. He further said, "Perhaps you should go somewhere else because, you know, people take on the personality of the pastor." This basically meant that the congregation would not accept me as a preacher either. I told him I would go when God told me.

After this, other people heard about my being called to the ministry, and they became upset with me. Then the spirit of intimidation came in. I soon found that if you are anointed with power, others will try to keep you quiet, keep you off church programs, and talk to everybody but you, even if you are standing next to them. Unfortunately, this behavior happens frequently among Christians.

I was called by God to preach in the spring of 1996 and remained at this Church for two more years. Then God spoke and said it was time to move on. Boy, was I glad to leave. I never looked back. I learned a lot from the people who hurt me. One thing about me is that when I move on, I move on. Any man, as Jesus recorded, "who puts his hands to the plow and looks back is not fit for the Kingdom." I don't nurse negativity or rehearse it; I let go and let God, then move on.

Being called to the ministry, as we know, is an awesome job and a tremendous and humbling experience, but there are three things that I encountered in the journey to climb Jacob's ladder. I call them the Trinity of the Enemy— the spirits of intimidation, jealousy, and envy.

People who are highly anointed will run into a lot of these kinds of spirits. Not too many people have been highly anointed by God. Some are just anointed with gifts but depending on the magnitude of the job, God has equipped some of us with much power—much required, much received. Ministry is not a glamorous position. It takes more than it gives. Also, you cannot tell God what you want or how much. He gives to you according to His perfect will.

Of all the spirits, intimidation is the worst because it combines jealousy and envy. The spirit of intimidation is very prevalent among believers. It can take a home, ministry, job, anything that was previously full of love, and change it all around. These, ladies and gentlemen are a part of the Trinity of the enemy. When people are fighting against one other, where is the first place you look? Who is running the show? Who is leading and managing the people? Can they be the problem and the reason for this division?

A body without a head is a freak. Improper leadership poisons the whole body. People placed in leadership positions, either out of their season or when they have not been called can cause many problems due to their lack of spiritual connection with God.

People who suffer from intimidation know the ex-perienced people. The persons with the knowledge and the spiritual power are those who can get the job done. Well, instead of using all this talent, these individuals constantly worry about someone trying to take their position. This often happens in marriages when a person feels threatened by a spouse.

People with sharpened skills like to see things move effectively. Experienced individuals have already encountered the ups and downs in a certain area, and they seek to avoid duplication and unnecessary problems. Remember, once you have experienced something that works, you should always try to pass it on but, when you do this, be careful to avoid hurting others' feelings.

Intimidators feel threatened and seek to degrade the character of others. This gives them a sense of security and control. I have found that these people set their own traps and draw problems to themselves. This is done in some cases almost immediately. Remember, this is a weakness, like anything else, and it is our job to help them help themselves. As leaders, it is a requirement, not an option for us to help people with problems such as intimidation. None of us have arrived, and we all need support and help with our own issues.

If someone tries to degrade you or assault your character after your first encounter, be careful and try to talk it over with the person, especially if this is your manager. If you do not handle this properly, the problem will build, and it will come out in your attitude toward the other person. Always make sure you have another mature non-gossiper with you during your meeting. This avoids misunderstandings and unnecessary arguments.

There are things to look for when confronted with the spirit of intimidation and things to avoid in order to keep the peace. If you are a person with great spiritual power, you must be sensitive and prayerful about these kind of people because your very presence makes them uneasy. Remember, this is not about you. Seeking to do what is right in the eyes of God is what this is really all about, and every believer, regardless of spiritual level should practice this. Use the tactics below in all areas of your life, such as home, Church, and work, to help you handle conflict situations.

1. After the first encounter and/or misunderstanding, the persons involved usually do not talk the problem over however, the intimidator will seek first to tell the people in authority things to degrade your character. Beware. Usually these types of people blow simple things out of proportion and everything is a crisis. Be patient. Try to talk it over with them in the presence of a seasoned, non-gossiper to see if there was something you did wrong.

2. Know that the person who has this weakness needs to be delivered, like all of us have to be delivered, from something or somebody. Ask God to use you to help this person get to the next level, even if you know he does not care for you. Remember, it's not about you but what God wants to do through you. Ask God to help you bless your enemies.

3. Do not get upset if you have purposely been overlooked for a project or promotion. People who have high skills and intellect will not be asked to help by people who have the spirit of intimidation, so do not be surprised. It takes a strong, humble person to ask someone to do something he knows he cannot do himself and not feel threatened. If you really would like to do the project or help, go to the person and ask for something to do. You may have to humble yourself so he can see some of your godly characteristics. This is how to win people over. We cannot change anyone but ourselves. Love is the only

thing that conquers people. You can catch more flies with honey than vinegar.

4. The intimidator will only speak to certain people and will try very hard to avoid you. Speak anyway. Do not—I repeat do not—lose your blessing because of someone else's weakness. Some may be threatened by your presence, but their real problem is that you are anointed.

5. If others start to treat you nasty or are cold to you for no apparent reason, be consistent and do not react or respond to their actions. You must remain the same when things around you may change. Stability brings credibility. Be steadfast and unmovable. Watch as well as pray!

6. Some intimidators may seek to poison others' minds about you because they really are hoping you will disappear, leave, or quit. Leaders such as these are toxic, and God will judge and remove them. If they are at your job, you must remain humble and wait on God to move them or you. Intimidated people always feel threatened by someone. Do not take it personally because they treat most of the people around them this way. This is the spirit that controls their thinking.

7. The intimidator uses other people to do his dirty work, so it will not appear as if it is coming from him. This is the oldest trick in the book; it has played out. The victim must make sure he is telling the truth. One never has to remember the truth; it's the lie that must be rehearsed. Have your house in order. The truth will always prevail.

8. The intimidator will not use input from the people who threaten him simply because it is coming from them. Never mind that what is being suggested is needed. What is more important is not improvement, but making sure the people they feel threatened by do not get any credit, promotion, or accolades. The bottom line is that the intimidator is upset that he did not think of it first. The reason he has not is that he has been using most of his energy in a negative way, and he has no room for the positive to flow through. Our minds and hearts must be open and pure so that we can effectively be used to help others.

9. People in charge are often identified by their ability to lead and show love to others. Even if a person does not have a lot of experience, he can succeed in life by having the right attitude. If you see that less than one percent of the people you are working with do not want to participate in your office or Church activities, this could be a warning sign. Intimidators hardly ever produce fruit. People follow people who have power and who can get the job done. Good leaders use as many people as possible to get the job done, trying not to leave anyone out or to form informal cliques.

As stated several times already, attitude determines how high we will go in life. Some people are not liked because they have something others want, such as clothes, money, homes, status, power, etc. People are attracted to those who are anointed and gifted. They want what the anointed have, but some go about trying to get it the wrong way.

There should be absolutely nothing anyone can do to you that degrades your character. My parents taught me a long time ago that I was somebody, and this was not based on things, but on morals and treating people the way I wanted to be treated. What some people think or do not think really does not mean anything. Always consider the source from which the information is coming and rise above the situation. Never stoop to a lower level. Love others unconditionally, and learn to move on, exemplifying Christlike characteristics. Be determined to do what's right. How can the devil compete with that?

Now that you have read about where I have been and my foundation, you will now see the woman I have become. Be open-minded and give me room to express the real Lillie. The following information is my testimony of how I obtain and remain focused while going through some of my life's personal struggles.

Chapter 15

Kept Woman Of Jesus (KWJ)
My Testimony

Throughout our Christian journey, we will be attacked often by other believers. Although, I love God's children, sometimes they can be the most unpleasant people on the face of the earth. The title of this chapter is definitely my testimony. Growing up without parents, many of us know is extremely hard, and trying to live right is extra hard. Being saved at the age of nine and beginning a ministry at nineteen exposed me to several encounters with God during my teenage years. I was always trying to please Him. No one can take away my intimate relationship with Him. I learned the art of what it means to be God's child. I also

93

learned that having Him early in life demonstrates that there is more to being young than making mistakes.

After my parents' death, all I had was God and my family; that was it. God, in my early teenage years, proved to me that He was with me and that He had a divine purpose and plan for my life. I always felt different and that I was living beyond my years.

God never let me go too far in what I wanted to do, but like any other teenager, I was curious. I wanted to experience some things, but God always stepped in. After I would go to a certain point, He would pull me back and say "That's enough." He would just not leave me alone.

I tried very hard during my teenage years to stay a virgin. I just could not see sleeping with anybody because I felt I was too young. This stemmed from my experiences with my mother bathing us and the things she would say about how precious our bodies were. I never forgot them.

While I was growing up, often youth and even grown people would come to me about their problems with life and relationships. I would always take them to the Bible to read what "thus saith the Lord." This advice-giving started for me at the age of fifteen. Although I was a virgin, I had some knowledge of what the Bible said about sex, love, relationships, and life. People wanted my advice mainly because I would always try to tell them the truth in love, as it related to God's Word, not always something they wanted to hear.

In addition to trying to keep my virginity, I also thought about becoming a nun once I graduated from high school. Well, that thought left me quickly when I met someone at nineteen who treated me well. Even in this relationship, God never let me go too far. It was always after I became sexually intimate that God came breaking up my relationships. I became sexually intimate late in life, and God cut it off quickly. I was never able to experience a full-fledged relationship with a man.

After entering the ministry, I decided to rededicate my life to Christ. I had been going to Church all along and never stopped, even while I was in college. But felt I needed to renew my vows from the age of nine and also because the devil was trying to distract me with men coming in my life. I knew I could not serve God and have a boyfriend, too so I broke up with him in that same year. At nineteen, my work for God became very serious to me, and I was truly honored and blessed. It was at this age that I started tithing with no job or real money; I just had limited funds from scholarships and seasonal part-time jobs. I also started fasting and praying. Thereafter, I went to another level in God.

The Church has always been a place of refuge, respect, and honor for me. I simply loved God's house and His people. It was at this point of my spiritual maturity that I really, really started serving God and the Church in every aspect. Men were still coming, and I wanted to compromise and have both God and the intimate relationship without marriage, thinking that God would understand. Well, He didn't.

I will never forget what happened at age twenty-two, when I gotten into another relationship. I often made my partners wait a long time for sexual intimacy. I figured if he was going to get "it," then he deserved it. But, I'll never forget at the age of twenty-two, I thought I was in love and once I became sexually intimate, God showed up. He came in and broke up the relationship. I knew it was God because He had broken up the last relationship, too. Even before God did this, I remember going to Church one Sunday morning after a night of sexual intimacy. I felt nasty once I walked into the Church. I was late that Sunday, and I was ushered to the front. Although I usually sat in the front, I did not want to sit there that day. At any rate, there I was sitting in the front of the Church thinking about what had happened the night before and knowing that I knew better.

I felt so horrible that I thought that I was burning the seat of the Church. I was so sure the seat was burning, I turned around to look up to see if I saw smoke. This truly was one of the worse experiences of my life. I promised God from that day forward that I would stop being sexually active and wait on Him. I said to myself that if this is what I am going to feel like the day after, I don't need it. Of course, God had already destroyed the relationship. The man left for the military, so my experiences with men have been something close to nothing. I only had an "appetizer" experience, and have been waiting for the meal ever since. It has not been easy through this journey of celibacy. Thank God that I started fasting and praying as a teenager. This has been my secret weapon against my flesh. This is how I became a Kept Woman of God for God was really keeping my body under His subjection and will.

During this time of struggling with relationships, the very interesting thing was that I did not miss sexual intimacy—companionship, yes, but not sexual intimacy—at least not all the time. God in His miraculous power took my emotions in this area, housed them inside me, and put them under lock and key. In other words, God was in control. Even when I tried not to be kept by Him and no longer wanted to be kept by Him, He still kept me while saying, "I am saving you for someone special. I am saving you for someone special." I would say, "Where is he?" I got no reply. Today I understand why God said this, but for a while I thought He was trying to keep me just for Himself.

In a nutshell, God never let me get away with anything because every time it looked like I was going in the wrong direction, things would start falling apart in my life, and I would get scared.

During my late twenties, I decided I was tired of this celibacy thing, and I was going to break it, whether God liked it or not. I knew exactly who to call. All day I was determined my celibacy was going to end. Fortunately, God blocked everything and spoke to me and said, "If you try this again, I will severely punish you." Believe me, I was scared to death and so thankful that He thought enough of me to keep me from falling into sin.

After not having sex for so long, and then having a fall would have been devastating. I would have felt worse than I did at age twenty-two when I thought I was burning the seat of the Church. I am so glad God kept me. He has carried me this far, and I have no intentions of turning back now this would be absolute foolishness. It would have to be by pure accident, not pre-meditated. Not giving in to your sexual desires is an everyday struggle you must take one day at a time.

I do know that whoever gets me is going to be very blessed, not just because of me saving myself, but because of who I am in God. He has made me a whole person through mind, body, and soul. I am not saying I am perfect or have arrived, but I am able, by my intimate relationship with God, to bring a healthy outlook and attitude to any kind of relationship.

My anointing, power, and virtue will be able to flow from my body to my mate's and to all those around me. Being prostrate before the Lord, naked but not ashamed, is how I have become whole in God. I have gotten everything in my life by lying on my stomach in prayer, not on my back with men. Knowing who you are in God is such a place of peace and stamina. Having identity in Jesus is just a good thing to have.

Through being obedient to God, He has preserved and reserved me. God has the ability to slow down aging and keep your mind and body fit. I didn't even see my twenties; I was too busy serving God, attending college and trying to help my family. I missed those years. Although, I am in my thirties, I feel now that I am really living my life in my twenties. I look about seven to ten years younger than my age, and my body has not had too much wear and tear. Avoiding running the streets, partying, and other things we do in excess with our bodies has really paid off for me. And, yes, I do take herbs and vitamins. I have been doing this for many years. I am a preventive-maintenance person and like to stay ahead of the game. Even the herbs and vitamins I take to help keep me healthy have been provided to me by God. He truly does supply all my needs.

Remember, a number is not the only thing that ages us. It is our experiences also that have a tendency to show up on us, especially our negative ones. Negative and other types of experiences that happen out of season or too soon in our lives often leave visible scars and make us show signs of aging quicker.

God has the ability to keep your emotions locked up. I am for real. I did not know what "being in heat" meant until I became twenty-five years old, and then God took it away at twenty-five. I guess He was trying to give me a taste of what it felt like. I learned at the age of twenty-nine what a "booty call" was after another female told me. So, God will really cover you, and He definitely has the power to keep your sexual potency locked up so that you do not feel anything, even on the days when you wish you could.

Now, of course, people can have sex whether they are in heat or not because there are other ways to get aroused. My point is that God kept my emotions so they would not overtake me. And, yes, of course, I still get the urge, even though God has my body under His subjection, but I do not get it every five minutes. As I have gotten older, I have learned how to handle my passions. The Bible calls this self-control. In other words, you know it's there, but it's not. God gives you the power to transcend the feelings. He keeps you busy so you burn the energy in other ways. Trust me on this one. You have a sense of your sexuality, but it is dormant and not fully activated. Now, it can become activated by being in the wrong place at the wrong time. The key is preventive maintenance and not trusting yourself but trusting God to keep you. God is a good Father because He knows how to keep us busy.

I have come this far by faith believing and leaning on the Lord, trusting in His Word, and He has never failed me yet. I do not try to test myself to see if I am strong by being in the wrong places. I just take one day and one moment at a time and ask God to help me hold on until my change comes. In doing so, I know myself and what I can and cannot handle during times of urges and vulnerability. I am true to myself and try to avoid things and people who will lead me into temptation.

As you continue to walk with God through a regime and life of fasting and praying, like Paul in the Bible, God will produce the fruit of the spirit, such as temperance and self-control in you. With this comes the gift of knowledge. Then wisdom follows.

Be careful, for the very thing that God blesses you with, the devil will try to steal. Over the years the devil knew, like so many others, that I had been kept and was waiting on God for my mate. I encountered a situation with people who did not know anything about me as a person. After all the years of waiting on God, the devil used people to try to challenge me. Can you imagine after saving myself for so long and going through all the struggles that it involve having someone imply that this is really not possible? I went to God about this and said, "The very thing about me that is considered to be a miracle in this day and age, that You have worked so hard on me about, someone has allowed the devil to try and steal." I further said to God, "You know I did this for You. I served You from a young age and tried extremely hard to be the woman of God You called me to be, by fasting and praying and denying my flesh of what Lillie wanted. All these years I have been suffering and waiting and waiting and suffering for You, through service and obedience. Of course, it has not been a perfect picture, but I know that through Your strength I have found favor in Your eyes. How could this happen to me? How dare someone disgrace You like that by talking about me in this regard?" God clearly spoke to me: "The battle is not yours but mine." He further said, "No weapon formed against thee shall prosper. It just will not work."

In every battle, God and I are going to win. God is always in it to win it, because it is already won. When people do not know you, they become curious, especially when they see your anointing and power. I think sometimes being economically stable and being a woman of honor makes jealousy, envy, and lies come in. The devil will use whomever he can.

Women who have been saving themselves for their mate like myself with almost no experience with men, look forward to the romance and lovemaking that comes with God's union. Women and even men who have had very sexually active lifestyles and get married with no time for renewal, often do not have too much to look forward to during the honeymoon. It is often just another vacation. But, for a virgin or a woman who has been celibate and set apart, it is an exciting and fulfilling time when mind, body, and soul can meet. Sexuality and spirituality are so tightly woven together that it truly is a divine connection.

Do not let anyone make you feel like you have a problem because you want to be married. Being married is a blessing from God. Just let God lead you in this area.

We all know it is not hard to get married, but staying together is the key. I could have been married twice before, but I chose to wait on whomever God had for me. I figured if God could give me good health, strength, warm blood running through my veins, air to breathe, a house, food, car, good career, etc., then He has enough wisdom and power to provide the right mate: a man who would love me as if God were loving me Himself. In other words, God would be loving me through my mate and vice versa.

If you are in a relationship that you are ashamed of due to fornication, ask God to help you and your partner become whole so you both can learn and embrace the art of true intimacy—which has nothing to do with physical connections or contact. This is when spirit and soul become one.

Two people who have been sexually active before marriage do not have the same things to look forward to as the couple who becomes sexually intimate after marriage. These are two different types of experiences. Seek to be kept by God, with the anticipation of divine intimacy that will come through a spiritual union with Him and then others, in that order. Don't forget to ask God to help you become whole in other areas of your life also.

When people's minds are negative, their thinking and actions follow. They travel the road of unsuccessfulness. The miracle is in our mouths, from the abundance of the heart, the mouth does speak. If you think a certain way, you speak a certain way, and you think other people think like you. We all must learn to keep our opinions to ourselves unless we are asked for them. Learn to stay out of other people's business since you have no idea what God may be trying to do through them. One would be surprised at what God has to go through to make people bring glory to His name. He uses back doors, windows, and cracks, and does whatever it takes to let us know that He loves us.

It's very interesting that the people who do the most talking are the biggest sinners. Whatever you tell others to do, it is always for you first. Do not get spiritual amnesia about your past and present situations. The devil uses people to take special interest in trying to destroy the character of others and the years of work and time God has invested in them. It is a slap in the face to God when someone tries to curse what He has done and continues to do through your life. God does carry us through so that we have a testimony to tell others about His awesome power. Never give people power over your life. Rebuke the unclean spirit in them and move on. You know the journey that God had to bring you through.

Now, after not being sexually active for so, so long, I look back and say, "Thank you, Jesus." (I'm saying this in tongues—my spiritual language.) It is truly a miracle from God how He kept me, and I know it is for a reason. My message is to all people, but particularly the young. They must understand and know that God has the ability and capability to keep them. God can do it. I really, really believe He kept me so I could write this book and share my testimony with others.

I remember, at the age twenty-five, I was ashamed to tell people I was saving myself for my mate because just about everyone I knew was sexually active. At this age, it was a big, big struggle, and I had so many successful men whom I considered five-star, who would do just about anything for me. Even at the age of twenty-seven, the one man I wanted, wanted to get married, and God said, "He's not the one." I was so mad at God, and I wanted Him to fix him up. God said, "Are you willing to wait for me to fix him up?" My reply was, "No." He was a little older than me, and I knew fixing him could take a long time because he was set in his ways. I have always liked older men who were established and mature like my father. Waiting on God to give you the one He has for you is the way to go, for He knows what's best for you. God sends or exposes us to His will, then we must choose to follow His greatness or to follow ourselves. The sum of our lives lies in the choices we make. Seek to choose wisely in every area of your life, and life will be rich and rewarding. Choose with a plan in your head and God in your heart, and you can never lose. When making decisions about marriage, remember: having a common past is good, for it unites your yesterdays. But, common goals are better, they unite your tomorrows.

103

When I did my dissertation, it was on the topic "God's Keeping Power." His ability and capability to keep us beyond our own comprehension is truly miraculous. So, if someone says they have been saving themselves sexually for their mate whether it's been one month or one year, do not give the credit to the devil by saying they must be funny or something. This is truly an insult to God, especially when it comes from other Christians. Just be honest that this is unfamiliar to you but not impossible for God.

Standing your ground and believing God in spite of the cost is the life of a believer. When we think about faith and its importance, we must know that we are the sum of all our experiences. In each level of life, through trials and tribulations, we get stronger as our level of faith grows. It's like a circle. Each time we get through something, we step out into the next level of the circle, which entails other challenges. (Benny Hinn) puts it very nicely when he says, "There is good faith, that is faith of a babe in Christ. There is great faith, faith of a growing Christian, and there's perfect faith that is unmovable faith, faith that, come hell or high water, you believe God all down in your toes." This, ladies and gentlemen, is the kind of faith I have, but my story has not been a fairy tale. This anointing has cost me a great deal of pain and sacrifice.

I believe God so much I cannot even tell people things He has told me because I know they just will not believe me. I can only share some things with people who have the kind of faith I do. I like to call it "crazy" faith. Believe me, God had to test me over and over, and life has not been a crystal ball. And, of course, I am still growing in the area of faith.

If God has told you something is going to happen in your life, such as a change in your career or family situation, just believe that He can achieve it. He delights Himself in those who believe all down in their toes that He is willing and able to do it. For without faith, it is impossible to please God.

Sometimes standing with Him, you must stand alone. I do not know how many times it seemed like God got me in trouble because I listened to Him. It appeared in the beginning that I must have been crazy, but after a while, He came right on time. God has often made me do and say things out of my character, things I really did not feel comfortable or accustomed to doing or saying. Of course, it's never been anything immoral, just out of the norm. Often, God charges us to do something that others view as a sign of weakness, like saying you are sorry for something somebody else has done to you.

Often with strong people, such as myself, God makes you bite the bullet about something for which another person should apologize. Being mature mentally and spiritually is a burden to carry. If the other individual is not where you are, it takes the mature person to keep things in harmony. Problems can never be solved through separation. People must come face to face to resolve issues. And, yes, the stronger and more mature person will have the responsibility of helping the other one come to another level in life, as he humbles himself to do or say things he would not normally say or do.

As mentioned, God has often had me tell people things I really was not comfortable telling them. I can still feel the piercing in my heart even today about the way God pricked my heart to do certain things.

Many times I felt He was making me tell people bad news or something they did not want to hear. But God said to me, "My Word is not 'bad news' but Good News." And, I have to say, I agree that God's Word is good for the soul and generates life, correction, and direction. When we give a person information, it is usually a confirmation of something they already know. I always tell people to take the information to the Lord in prayer and let God give you insight. Information brings revelation. God often creates a situation for revelation so that He can reveal Himself through that circumstance or situation.

Giving information or prophetic words to people should be backed up with scripture. God will give you a Rhema word so the person will know that this is from God and not from your flesh. A Rhema word is one from God that speaks specifically to your present situation.

After being obedient to God and stepping out on faith and out of my tradition, I could see how God used me in several situations to inform people of things to come in their lives. I take great pride in watching them grow and knowing that I had something to do with helping them reach another level. All this came from my obedience to God's command.

As stated, information brings revelation, which is needed to cut down confusion that may be around us. Light and darkness cannot dwell in the same place. This is why I tell people never to cut off their ears because you never know. Take whatever people tell you to God and let Him bring it to light. Again, if someone tells you something, this does not mean you must act on it today or tomorrow. It is to inform you so that you have the right data about a situation. Then pray on it and let God handle it.

Those in the ministry know that ministry takes more than it gives, but we must be able to endure the rigor. The race is not given to the swift but those who can endure. In other words, you must be able to take a licking and keep on ticking; rise under fire.

In order to cross the Jordan River and reach the other side, the flesh must die. The Jordan River was one in the Bible that many wanted to cross in order to obtain their spiritual blessing. Crossing to the other side was a metaphor that was used about the river because there were so many things that happened in or around it. Jesus' baptism was one. One can often tell strong Christians from the weak ones who never take risks and always play it safe. They never want to rock the boat and just be easy come and easy go. But, when we think about how this country was founded, it is very evident that there was a lot of war before peace. In the end there will be much war before peace comes. Of course, I am not saying for you to be a troublemaker but, if you believe something is wrong, you cannot only pray about it, you must do something as well.

Prayer is an action word that means when you get off your knees, something is supposed to happen. After you pray the question should be, now what? Are you a part of the problem or part of the solution? No, I am not saying to fight every battle but that you should pick them. I know of so many things I had to go through in life—like swallowing my pride and being ridiculed due to lies and misunderstandings that weak people who do not want to come out of their comfort zone would not have survived.

Some of us, have been called to come out of the boat to walk on the water. Others have a special place in kingdom building. I firmly believe to whom much has been given, much is required. No deposit, no return. Little in, little out. Some weak people often think I am a troublemaker but it's not that. I don't go along with something just to say I am going along. I don't pick fights, but I do not run from them either. I love to see progression and progress. I will admit that I do need more patience with people, but when others tell me or act like they are so anointed, I expect more. But, most of the time, I find their anointing is not activated, and that's why they have no power to make things happen. This often happens due to sin, it's not your season to operate in this area, or this is just not your calling.

I have the ability to nurture people into wholeness. Love is the only thing that changes people. You cannot change anybody but yourself. As you love people, you love unconditionally, and this helps others move into wholeness. The strong must bear the infirmities of the weak. The same comfort of healing God gave me over my parents' death, I am now able to share with others. I have been ordained by God with this special anointing to help the brokenhearted and those who struggle with saving themselves sexually for their mates. I have the power not just to break those yokes but to destroy them. I also have the power to help those who need to recover and heal from the broken hearts of childhood pain before it turns into adult insanity.

As we love and forgive, God can help and deliver us, which sets us free to help others who are bound by circumstances and the spirit of unforgiveness. It's hard to help people until you have first helped yourself, although it is not impossible for hurting people to help others. One must be very careful and use wisdom, because usually you will find hurting people hurt people.

For me, learning to fast and pray early in life is what saved me over the years. We all must be careful because our flesh is tricky and fickle. It wants to be pampered, fed, and touched. I am very, very good to myself and believe in the ultimate pampering—getting my feet massaged, which is my favorite; then aromatherapy bath; fine dining; and body massages. But I've learn, we must, from time to time, tell the flesh "no," especially when we see it getting out of hand.

We are all creatures of habit and must deviate from pleasures from time to time. This creates balance and room for correction with a renewal process that can only come from God. In fasting, you are putting your flesh under subjection and simply saying "no" to it. By praying and reading God's word, you are not filling your flesh up with pizza or something but with God's power and spirit. It is truly a miracle that after a consistent regime of this, it will become a lifestyle. It is a holistic way of living because it covers all the parts of the person: mind, body, soul, spirit, and fleshly desires.

Fasting for the mind keeps us focused; fasting for the body gives self-control and it renews the soul. Fasting with the spirit feeds it God's Word, and with the flesh, it teaches balance. Saying no to excessive food is truly the way to keep your weight manageable. I consider eating to be the ultimate luxury in life, but we all need self-control. I have noticed in the past that when I slack up in my fasting, my eating increases so much that I could try to eat a whole pizza. Yes, little ol' me. I had to tell my flesh out loud while walking around in the house, "No. You cannot have this. Now leave me alone." Mind you, I was talking to myself. It was almost as if the pizza was calling me. My flesh tried to do this with ice cream, too. Guess what kind? Breyers Butter Pecan or Almond. It must be Breyers and it must be Butter Pecan or Almond. I won't look at anything else. And, yes, I got this from my daddy, who always ate ice cream.

In "Lessons For Living, Part 2" in the back of this book page 141, I have provided the secrets to my success on Fasting and Praying. Now I know everyone reading this book may not be spiritually educated, but my godparents always said, "Whatever you want the most, give it up." If you want love, give love; if you want money, give money. It is more blessed to give than to receive. The world says take, take, take, but God says give, give, give. When planting seeds, whether good or bad, you will reap what you have sown. God looks at our willingness to do something. We may not agree with Him or think what He is doing is right, but being obedient and having a willingness to yield to His way is what pleases Him the most.

Chapter 16

My Ministry, My Purpose, My Passion To Serve Jesus

My ministry, my purpose, and my passion to serve all add up to my life of work and service for the Kingdom. It is my designed desire to serve God to my fullest capacity. I have been serving Him for so many years; I would not be able to function if I did not. I have learned over the years the different areas and ways to serve God. I know that your family is your first ministry. My initial time of service came with my mother as a young child. I saw her help so many people over the years. By serving others I learned a valuable lesson about sharing and giving.

My mother knew that she would not see us when we got older. She often made comments while we were helping her with community projects saying, "I am not going to see you kids when you get older, but I am planting seeds now with the hope that one day somebody will help you." I never really knew why she talked like this, but now I know. She knew the kind of man she married.

My mother planted seeds for her children many years ago by helping so many people. I am happy to say that God saw and heard her plea. As a result of her service, a small park located in Philadelphia, Pennsylvania, was named in her honor, the late and great Lillie C. Coley.

As I look back over my life of service and all the things I did in the community and church, I am so, so grateful that each and every one of my experiences has helped me in service today.

Getting my foundation and skills to serve from my home and from my hometown church, Zion Baptist Church, under Rev. Leon H. Sullivan and Pastor Gus Roman, has helped me become the woman I am today. My parents and my church helped me bring forth my gifts and talents. My main gift was teaching. My parents saw this in me at the age of nine from my communication skills and helped me to utilize it. My father went out to buy me a chalkboard, and my mother went to my school and got me old textbooks so I could have classroom sessions at home. I taught my brothers and sisters just about every day. As I got older my gift grew stronger. Even when I was not really ready for certain things, my parents built me up so much that I believed that I could do anything. I truly have come from a five-star Church and family.

As I look at where I am today, I truly cannot believe how far God has brought me and the many blessings He has bestowed upon me. But, as we all know, it is never about us, but what God wants to do through us. For all the people who hurt me and did things to me that were not of God, I want to thank you because it made me a better and wiser person.

When God expanded my ministry to other states, I experienced some trials and tribulations but I was prepared for each and every test of faith. I had a prerequisite lesson for these trials in my previous life and Church. God laid out the stepping stones. I can honestly say that I am applying my previously established principles to handling my present situation and circumstances.

Truly, God has prepared me fully for service and dealing with all types of people, regardless of their status and level in life. Even with my passion to serve, I know there is a price to pay. I have come this far by faith. As I write this, I am so sensitive and in tune to my purpose for God that I will not let anyone turn me away. It has been through God that I have been able to embrace myself and give a helping hand to others.

My organization, Community Empowerment Outreach, started out as a ministry, but God expanded it to include other services to help the entire individual. We have a holistic approach to love and help people into wholeness.

Knowing my purpose and destiny, I am excited and delighted to be used by the Lord for He has told me ministry is all about bearing more and more fruit. Because fruit produces fruit, this also applies to vegetables as well. For example, if you start out planting one apple, one orange, or one potato, when it grows you end up with so much more.

One apple has five to seven seeds that can be replanted to continue the cycle. One orange comes with about ten seeds that can be replanted to continue the cycle, and one potato can produce at least five others. So, fruit produces more fruit. Vegetables produce more vegetables. Planting them in the right soil with the proper amount of water, sun, and loving care brings life.

I have provided some information that can help any of us to produce the right outcome or fruit when doing Kingdom work. It is located in the "Lessons for Living, Part 3" on page 142.

Remember, it is not about you but what God wants to do through you. So, when people hurt you, especially those close to you, don't get discouraged. The enemy often uses people to try to discourage us so that we, in turn, will not bear more fruit.

God uses the good, the bad, and the ugly circumstances to cause production in our lives. This is the methodology and ideology of God. Do not try to figure it out, just trust Him. Be an overcomer stay focused and determined while keeping your eyes on the prize.

Whatever you need or want to achieve, God's got it. He's able to do everything but fail. Learning to trust God and not myself has been the greatest lesson in my life. Trust and believe—that's how you will succeed. Know that whatever you have been through, none of your experiences have been wasted. This is one of the many things I love about God. He uses all things to help us grow, whether by accident or on purpose. When we trust Him we can rest in His bosom and know everything happens for a reason. God is truly too wise to make a mistake.

Next you will see the different characters of God. Discover God's track record to learn how He is viewed throughout the entire Bible while comparing Him in your own life. He is the same God yesterday, today, and forever more. Rejoice in knowing that this is the kind of God we serve. Who would not serve a God like that? Taste and see that the Lord is good, and yes, He gets sweeter than the day before. For me, God has been so many things, but, the main thing God has been in my life is a keeper.

Names of God Throughout the Entire Bible

In Genesis He is a Creator

> Exodus
> > Deliverer/Keeper and Sustainer

> Leviticus
> > Eternal Sacrifice

> Numbers
> > Trusted Guide

> Deuteronomy
> > Redeeming Prophet

> Joshua
> > Captain of Our Salvation

> Judges
> > Steadfast Judge and Lawgiver

> Ruth
> > Kinsman Redeemer

> Samuel
> > Interceding King

> II Samuel
> > Anointed King

My Story

I Kings
   Wise King

II Kings
   Reigning King

I Chronicles
   Sovereign King

II Chronicles
   Glory of the Lord

Ezra
   Faithful Scribe

Nehemiah
   Rebuilder

Esther
   Hidden Teacher

Job
   Dayspring and Faithful One

Psalms
   Shepherd and Song Maker

Proverbs
   Wisdom

Ecclesiastes
   Only Hope

Song of Solomon
   The Bridegroom

Isaiah
   Prince of Peace

Jeremiah
   Righteous Branch and Friend

Lamentations
>Weeping Prophet

Ezekiel
>Watchman and Wheel in the Sky

Daniel
>Rescuer

Hosea
>Faithful Husband

Joel

>God's Outpouring of the Holy Spirit

Amos
>Burden Bearer

Obadiah
>Highest Authority

Jonah
>God's Mercy

Micah
>Messenger of the Gospel

Nahum
>Avenger of God's Elect

Habakkuk
>Firm Foundation

Zephaniah
>Prince of Peace and Glory of Israel

Haggai
>Restorer of God's Lost Heritage

Zechariah
>Merciful Father

Malachi
   Glorious Promise

Matthew
   King of the Jews

Mark
   Son of God and Wonder Worker

Luke
   Son of Man

John
   Word Made Flesh

Acts
   Power on High

Romans
   Salvation and Justifier

I Corinthians
   Gift of the Spirit

II Corinthians
   Victory

Galatians
   Liberator

Ephesians
   Chief Cornerstone

Philippians
   Provider and Supplier

Colossians
   Fullness of God

I Thessalonians
   Soon Coming King

II Thessalonians
Messiah

I Timothy
Mediator

II Timothy
Faithful Witness

Titus
Faithful Pastor and Blessed Hope

Philemon
Friend that is Closer than a Brother

Hebrews
High Priest

James
Great Physician

I Peter
Chief Shepherd

II Peter
Saviour

I John
Righteousness

II John
Everlasting Love

III John
Truth

Jude
Majesty and Power

Revelation
King of Kings and Lord of Lords

Chapter 17

My Story:
"No One Can Tell-It Like I Can Tell-It"

I needed to write this book for three reasons. First, I did not go through all I went through to keep it to myself. It is profound and prophetic that God uses our experiences to help others throughout life. It has been twenty-four years since my parents' death, and God knew that I was going to *need,* not want, to share my story at such a time as this. God is so dynamic and strategic that He allowed a tragedy to take place because He knew that during my journey through life someone would need to hear it to become healed. The people we come in contact with in life and the places we go have

121

been planned. Our lives is a great big set-up facilitated through the power and mind of God.

We love to try to find our way out of trouble but if we never have problems, how will we know that God can solve them? He creates situations for revelation so He can reveal Himself to us. My family's' tragedy did turn into an opportunity. It gave my family and me time to share without being in despair. We must all learn to tell our story, because nobody can tell it like we can tell it. When you talk about something negative with a positive attitude, it provides a healthy outlet. Through this restoration comes regeneration, which results in rejuvenation for higher determination.

Young people must be aware of and conscious that life will, and I repeat, will, bring troubles. But how we handle our troubles is what dictates our future. Remember, life's outcome is ten percent trouble and ninety percent how you handle it.

All of the proceeds from this book will be donated to my organization's community projects to help young people, particularly those who are going through or have gone through, trauma during their teenage years. My siblings and I will tell them our story and give them tactics to help them become overcomers in life. Two of the projects will be called Youth Empowerment Services (Y.E.S.) and Controlling Our Own Lives (C.O.O.L.). Also, we will support local churches' community projects that focus their activities on youth and young adults.

These services will seek to help individuals with social and economic empowerment because it is very hard to succeed by yourself, especially without the support of parents who, if they are responsible, will do everything in their power to help their child. But, if a child has no parents, he or she in some cases must conquer the world alone.

We will seek to make this journey a little easier for youth who plan to reach higher levels in life. We will provide technical direction and direct assistance to help them achieve their goals in life.

Life is so much more worth living when you know you are not alone and someone is there to help. Our youth will learn the art of being victors and not victims.

The second reason I had to write this book is so that people will know the truth about me firsthand, rather than hearing it from others. Sometimes, when people find out information about your past, they mess up your story when trying to tell it to others. God ordained me to write this book so others could see His awesome power and love for my family. The same love He gave me, He can give you. I did not want a busybody to try to mess up my story. My story is for all people who need hope and assurance that a new day is dawning. Who would have ever thought that God could do this for me? He allowed me to go to college and earn four degrees in spite of all I went through and encountered in life. I am truly grateful and forever thankful for all that He has done. If I can finish college and succeed, anybody can do it.

The third reason I had to write this book was to clear my father's name. No, I am not making excuses for what he did. I would never do that. But, I wanted people to know that some good things and people, unfortunately, can have a bad ending. The sad part about this is that the tragedy could have been prevented if someone had helped my father with his unresolved issues as I am trying to help people now.

My father was a good man who loved his family. He will not have a chance to live his life over, but I think he can rest in peace knowing that his family has forgiven him and will always, always love him.

Please, please seek help for all the hurts and pains. Take care of them like you would take care of other areas of your life. Unresolved issues do nothing more than get worse over time. You are not in your situation alone. There is somebody somewhere who is going through something similar. Seek help because it is the right thing to do, and do not worry about what people think. Ask God to deliver you from people and their negative opinions. Seek to be around those who will not poison or vex your spirit but *build you up*. You need others for encouragement and correction in love.

Being free in your mind from carrying unnecessary weight is really the life you want to live. Otherwise, you will be enslaved to yourself, and your problems will mentally weigh you down. Destruction usually follows along with a life of unfulfillment. Please seek help until you find it, and continue to knock until a door is opened to you. After every no there is a yes somewhere.

I am particularly proud of my brothers and sisters who, to this very day, are being kept by God. God did not just keep me, He kept my family. God does not just save individuals, He saves a nation. By keeping all of us, God kept an entire generation and those who will follow us. If the devil had his way, we would have been wiped from the face the earth. What the devil meant for evil, God meant for good.

My brothers, as I have stated, have never been to jail. My sisters had no teenage pregnancies. They all still live as good citizens. Of course, everything is not perfect, but it could be much worse. We have been kept by the hand and power of

God and God alone. How God kept my family and me was a part of His divine providence and was strategically orchestrated by Him. We were never separated from one another or lost in the system that handles wards of the state. We remained in our family home which was purchased by our father, until we were ready to move out.

Our parents raised us from the cradle and from their graves. Though we had legal guardians who were members of our family, we just followed the traditions and manners that our parents taught us as if they were still alive. This was their legacy. And yes, we're grateful for all the family members who helped us as we were growing up.

As we continue to walk by faith and not by sight, it is then that we can continue to march on to see what the end will bring. We went through all this hell in order to help others down the road.

Who would have ever thought that something so negative and hurtful could turn into such an opportunity? This tragedy did in fact turn into an opportunity to share with the entire world the fact that we can rise above our circumstances and make it, in spite of our troubles. As mentioned, from these experiences came the birth of my organization, Community Empowerment Outreach (CEO), which is designed to help individuals make it through tragedies and disappointments in life. In an effort to touch all people from all walks of life, this book has been translated initially into six other languages. In addition, it will be available in Braille and audio. Other supporting materials, such as daily devotionals, a healing journal and tips on how to live a life kept by God are also available.

As a result of living for God young, most of my major accomplishments happened by the age of twenty-five and thirty. I am now enjoying the fruits of my labor while waiting on God to take me to the next level in life.

Seek to live under God's keeping power, which gives us the ability to live to our fullest potential. Also, try to live a life of pure faith in spite of the cost, for this is what moves God to work diligently on our behalf. Now, I look at my situation and say, "Look at me. I'm testimony. I did not make it on my own, but somebody prayed for me, and I learned to hold on." Look for my brothers, sisters, and me—even some of my nieces and nephews— as we go around the world to share our story to help encourage others not to become victims of their circumstances. God bless you, and may heaven continually shine upon you.

See our family photos on the following pages!!!

**Andrew(deceased)
with a friend**

Edward and James

Lillie and Frank

Kurt

We Are A Family

Front L-R—Shirl, Michelle,
Edward, Yvette,
Back L-R—Kurt, Frank, Annette,
James, Joesph

Next Generation—Nieces and Nephews

Next Generation—Nieces and Nephews

We Are A Family

Next Generation—Nieces and Nephews

Next Generation—Nieces and Nephews

Lesson For Living-Part 1

God's Way to Gain and Maintain Wealth

Plans fail for lack of counsel, but with many advisers
they succeed.
—Proverbs 15:22 (NIV)

It is the will of God for you to continue to experience
financial increase so that the vision of the Lord may
go forward and abound!

Wealth gotten by vanity shall be diminished: but he
that gathereth by labour shall increase.
— Proverbs 13:11 (KJV)

God has promised to bless the work of our hands
through our ministry and servanthood.

Many of you who are reading this have tremendous
visions for the nation, and your financial wherewithal
is not presently commensurate to your destiny.

What do you do when you've been given an
assignment from the Lord that is far greater than your
present resources? Do you know that you can be
given a divine responsibility that will cause your faith
to increase, and thereby, bring pleasure to God? For
without faith, it is impossible to please Him.
(Hebrews 11:6 NIV)

We must keep our ministries moving in faith in every
realm. I want to suggest some principles that will
assist you in bringing forth the harvest of finance that
is absolutely essential in these last days.

1. Accept that your assignment is greater than your present financial situation. When Jesus commanded the multitudes to be fed, there was not enough to feed them. Their assignment exceeded the amount of money in the treasury. Quit struggling. It's time to move on now and step out on faith!

2. God specializes in the impossible. If something is currently within your scope, it will not require faith and you can get the glory. But if this assignment is from God, and He has to do it, then God will get the glory. But Jesus beheld them, and said unto them, "With men this is impossible; but with God all things are possible." (Matthew 19:26 KJV) *With God.....you can!*

3. Enter into the power of prayer. Jeremiah in the Bible says to call on God. You can pray and receive what you need. Jesus taught in his model prayer to pray for provision.

4. Rehearse the Laws of Sowing and Reaping. Usually, harvest is determined at seed time. If you sow bountifully, you can expect to reap bountifully.

5. Maintain a biblical confession of faith for God's continued financial increase. Remember it was the Holy Ghost who inspired the following verses: "And Jesus answering saith unto them, Have faith in God." — (Mark 11:22 KJV)
"For verily I say unto you, that whosoever shall say unto this mountain, be thou removed, and be thou cast into the sea; and shall not doubt in his heart, but shall believe that those things which he saith shall come to pass; he shall have whatsoever he saith." —(Mark 11:23 KJV); "Therefore I say unto you,

What things whatsoever ye desire, when ye pray, believe that ye receive them, and ye shall have them." —(Mark 11:24)

6. Find a person to stand in faith with you. There is power in the prayer of agreement. (Matthew 18:19 KJV) The strong can hold up the weak.

7. Make sure your house is in order. Many times, our natural life is lacking in Divine Order.

Get ready for God's provision to match your vision! (Proverbs 29:18 KJV)

If you are following the vision of the Lord, He will give you a plan. Begin to follow others who have had success in releasing finances for ministry. Money follows ministry. Get to work and concentrate on God's provision. Favor is attracted to you because you follow God's plan of action. God is able to make all grace abound to you!

And, having been set free from sin, you have become the servants of righteousness of conformity to the divine in thought, purpose, and action. (Romans 6:18 NIV)

Develop a right attitude toward money in ministry.

People rarely go farther than their leadership. Don't put yourself in a position where debt governs your life and ministry. (Romans 13:8 NIV)

Don't ever allow the devil to steal from you. (John 10:10 NIV) The greatest battles are fought in the mind. God is not short of money. God has given you the power to get wealth in order to establish His covenant.

Don't you know that I have the resources for this, says the Lord. I have not planned your life, only to leave out what you need to accomplish my plans. I am more than this.

Lesson For Living-Part 2

Fasting and Praying—Weapons of Your Warfare

"But when you fast, put oil on your head and wash your face, so that it will not be obvious to men that you are fasting, but only to your Father, who is unseen; and your Father, who sees what is done in secret, will reward you openly." Matthew 6:17-18 KJV

What Is Fasting?

One of the most powerful weapons of spiritual warfare that God has given to His children is fasting—a way of crucifying the flesh or denying your flesh the basic sustenance of food. Although fasting will weaken you physically, it will highly enlighten you spiritually. Fasting is a form of spiritual discipline that informs God that you are serious about repentance. It is a significant part of your Christian walk, just as praying and reading the Bible are. Fasting is for everyone who desires to draw closer to God.

When you fast, you do not have to give up just food; it can be anything of importance to you that is a sacrifice. Whenever you fast, you need to pray and seek the Lord, otherwise you are just depriving your body of food and not getting in touch with what the Holy Spirit is trying to tell you.

Although fasting is not commanded in the Bible, it is expected of all believers in their Christian walk, for Matthew 6:17-18 says, "When you fast. " Jesus did not say, "if you fast," but rather "when you fast," therefore, Jesus reveals through scripture that fasting is expected however, it is not commanded. You are not committing sin by not fasting.

Lesson For Living-Part 3

Bearing Fruit

Have you noticed that there seems to be a huge emphasis on spiritual gifts today? You hardly ever hear of anyone talking about spiritual fruit anymore. While I believe spiritual gifts serve an important purpose in the Body of Christ, I want you to be equally (if not more) aware of the fruit of the Holy Spirit and how important it is to understand what God is doing in your own life. The ministry of the Holy Spirit manifesting His fruit in us is far more important than spiritual gifts. Many people continue to seek the power and manifestation of the gifts of the Spirit, but they do not place a priority on the call of every believer to a holy life. Our desire should be to seek earnestly "the Giver and not the gifts," then "all these things (Christlike qualities) shall be added unto you" through the supernatural power of the Holy Spirit. (Matthew 6:33 NIV)

Regardless to what anyone says, God still frowns on sin, and He has called Christians to be conformed to the image of His dear Son. We, as Christians, need to be properly rooted in prayer and in the Word of God so we can bear spiritual fruit.

I find it quite fascinating that the Bible both begins and ends talking about fruit. God's divine purpose for your life is for you to bear spiritual fruit. Your relationship to Jesus is described in John 15:5 in this way: "He is the vine, and we are the branches."

In John 15:16, the Bible declares, "Ye have not chosen me, but I have chosen you and ordained you, that ye should go and bring forth fruit, and that your fruit should remain: that whatsoever ye shall ask of the Father in my name, he may give it to you."

In order to bear this fruit, you must be planted and properly rooted spiritually. If you want to bear spiritual fruit, then you must reject sin, walk in holiness, and delight in God's law. You must also be planted in the house of God connected to the body of Christ. Bearing fruit is a supernatural process. Jesus produces the fruit and we bear it. The Father is the Divine Gardener who supervises the process.

The purging process is one that many Christians reject because when they go through difficulties in their lives, they always think that the devil is attacking them. God prunes productive plants for the same reason a farmer prunes—to produce more fruit. Jesus' parable of the barren tree in Luke 13:6-9 NIV illustrates how God works continually and patiently with the unproductive to produce fruit.

The Nine Fruits

The Book of Galatians identifies the Christlike qualities that God wants to produce in our lives: "But the fruit of the Spirit is love, joy, peace, longsuffering, gentleness, goodness, faith, meekness, temperance: against such there is no law."

—Galatians 5:22-23 KJV

Notice that the "fruit" of the Spirit is singular, for there is one fruit revealed in nine separate supernatural manifestations:

The first three focus on our relationship with God.

The second three fruits focus on your relationship with others.

The final three fruits focus directly on the individual.

Love

Joy

Peace

Longsuffering

Gentleness

Goodness

Faith

Meekness

Temperance

These nine manifestations of the fruit of the Holy Spirit enable you to eliminate spiritual barrenness, to escape the corruption of the world, and to become partakers of the divine nature of God.

Believers, beware! There are many people out there wearing sheep's clothing who are "prophesying" by using divination. These people may appear to be holy; have their Christian bumper sticker; and know all the right phrases, like "Amen," "Hallelujah," "Glory to God," and "Praise the Lord!" but watch out, because they might just be ravening wolves.

References

Names of God, p. 115

Lessons for Living, Part 1: God's Way to Gain and Maintain Wealth, p. 137

Lessons for Living, Part 2: Fasting and Praying- Weapons of Your Warfare, p. 141

Lessons for Living Part 3: Bearing Fruit, p. 143

Portions of information taken from the "Growing Believer" Web site.

About the Author

Dr. Lillie M. Coley is a motivational/inspirational speaker who has worked in the community for more than fifteen years. She owns and operates a nonprofit organization, Community Empowerment Outreach (CEO), which focuses on working with youth and adults across the country on empowerment and economic issues.

She has a Bachelor of Science (B.S.) and a double major in computer science and math from Temple University. Her Master of Science (M.S.) studies were at Eastern College and Thomas Edison with Thomas Edison being the awarding institution. She then completed her doctoral studies at Philadelphia College of Bible in Vineland, New Jersey, and International Theological Seminary (ITS) with ITS being the awarding institution. Her last degree was completed by the age of thirty-two.

She is very active in the community, working on various boards where she shares an overall strategic plan of helping this nation to build a better family unit. Strong families means a stronger country. She recently was named Who's Who in the national registry and is a member of NAFE (National Association of Female Executives).

Dr. Coley has proven that one does not have to be a victim of his circumstances but we all must learn to rise above any situation, turning tragedy into opportunity through and by the power of God's love. She feels if she can finish college and start a business, anybody can in spite of what they have been through.

My Story will be available around the world and initially translated into six other languages. Other inspiring materials such as daily devotional readings, T-Shirts, and tips on how to live a life kept by God are now available. Watch Dr. Coley's Web site **(www.drlil.com)** for more details.

For more information about Community Empowerment Orgainzation, to book Dr. Lillie M. Coley, PhD for speaking engagements, or to receive additional copies of *My Story,* please contact one of the following:

Email: ceo1@mail.com

KWJ & CEO Publishing
609-225-6357

or

Write to:

P.O. Box 203
Blackwood, NJ 08012

Check Website(www.drlil.com) for up to date contact information.

All contributions may be made payable to:
"CEO-My Story"

www.ingramcontent.com/pod-product-compliance
Lightning Source LLC
LaVergne TN
LVHW021457080426

835509LV00018B/2315